GRAND STRATEGY AND THE RISE OF CHINA

Made in America

Zeno Leoni

agenda
publishing

To early-career researchers. May they write about what they want as opposed to what they must.

First published in 2023 by Agenda Publishing

Agenda Publishing Limited
PO Box 185
Newcastle upon Tyne
NE20 2DH
www.agendapub.com

ISBN 978-1-78821-601-2 (hardcover)
ISBN 978-1-78821-602-9 (paperback)

British Library Cataloguing-in-Publication Data
A catalogue record for this book is available from the British Library

Typeset by JS Typesetting Ltd, Porthcawl, Mid Glamorgan
Printed and bound in the UK by 4edge

GRAND STRATEGY AND THE RISE OF CHINA

Business with China

Series Editor: Kerry Brown

The titles in this series explore the complex relationship between Chinese society and China's global economic role. Exploring a wide range of issues the series challenges the view of a country enclosed in on itself, and shows how the decisions made by Chinese consumers, the economic and political choices made by its government, and the fiscal policies followed by its bankers are impacting on the rest of the world.

Published

Belt and Road: The First Decade
Igor Rogelja and Konstantinos Tsimonis

China's Hong Kong: The Politics of a Global City
Tim Summers

Grand Strategy and the Rise of China: Made in America
Zeno Leoni

The Future of UK–China Relations: The Search for a New Model
Kerry Brown

Contents

Preface and acknowledgements

China is a huge country, with a very long history, and an increasingly global influence. The implications of its domestic and foreign policies are far-reaching. Tracking everything China is or does is a mammoth task and most observers tend to do so by focusing on a specific research area or a specific angle. I am not different in this regard.

The perspective I have used to look at China follows my professional story of the last few years. It is based on an underlying claim, which might well be the most important statement in this book: it is not possible, I argue, to study modern and contemporary China in isolation from its relationship with the West. This is because China's struggles and successes over the last two centuries are closely linked to western policy towards China – at the same time, the rise of a western-led global economy, and the end of the Cold War might not have been possible without China. Studying China through the lenses of its relationship with the West means approaching this subject with a pragmatic – strategic – logic, rather than for the sake of knowing more about China.

This is the perspective that I have developed over the last four years and that has informed this book. From an academic point of view, my interest in China began with my PhD at the Department of European and International Studies, King's College London where I completed my thesis on US–China relations. More specifically, my objective was to analyse the foreign policy of the Obama administration towards China, applying a Marxist theory of imperialism, which involved looking at American grand strategy from a critical perspective. Between 2017 and 2018, between the final stage of my PhD and my first year of a full-time job, I realized I wanted to focus more on the Chinese perspective of the relationship. First, when studying the logic of the Washington

Consensus, I realized that I needed a better appreciation of what was behind American disappointment towards China. I found an answer to this question, eventually, by exploring in depth the symbiotic – nationalistic – relationship that exists in the PRC between the state and society, in particular between the state and the strategic industries.

Second, when I took my first full-time job in the Defence Studies Department at King's, I realized that China as an area of study was not, beyond the obvious narrow circles, as popular as it deserved to be. I recall the words of a report published by the think tank Mountbatten Society, which as late as early winter 2018 argued that the average British military chief is "China-blind". Therefore, thanks also to the valuable advice of my colleague Dr Warren Chin, I decided to take the opportunity to teach a China-focused module to colonels and generals of the Higher Command and Staff Course, a Five Eyes-focused career-development course delivered at the Defence Academy of the United Kingdom. Since then, I have gone on to develop modules and teaching material for a series of other courses across the Defence Studies Department. In reality, this lack of interest in China was not just the military's fault. It was a UK- and West-wide problem, and one of the implications of a so-called "strategic pause" in the post-Cold War years. The West was curious about China only in so far as it provided a profitable market. Then suddenly interest in China exploded towards the late 2010s, which provided a third reason for me to focus on China. The demand for China-focused knowledge was like an avalanche. Suddenly, we needed to deconstruct the China enigma and explain it to citizens and voters, across British and Italian media outlets. At times, this led to engagement with military institutions and policy-makers across different branches of the UK government, as well as the governments of Italy, Canada, Indonesia and Lithuania.

Along this journey, which has felt like completing a second PhD degree, I have met fascinating people in unexpected ways with whom I have had friendly exchanges of opinions, from a government official working on national security and China, to a Chinese defence attaché in London, and from a former British consul general in Hong Kong to a board member of the European Union chamber of commerce in Shenzhen, among many others. Eventually, these events led me to a joint appointment between the Defence Studies Department of King's College

London based within the Defence Academy of the UK and the Lau China Institute – also at King's College London. This position shared between an institution technically integrated within the security substructures of the US-led sphere of influence, and a department whose core business is to understand and open the China box to the world – not necessarily to justify what China does – accurately reflects my research interests and expertise. This has led me to study Sino-western relations in – hopefully – an unbiased fashion, trying to acknowledge the pros and cons of both worlds.

There seems to be, however, something absurd about claiming to academically span both worlds today. China and the West – especially the US – have increasingly been dissatisfied with the post-Second World War liberal order. In recent years they have considered the possibility of decoupling from one another, and the Covid-19 pandemic and the war in Ukraine have given both camps more tools and reasons to pursue such an objective. The world order might be on the verge of an Iron Curtain 2.0 that will be a more fine-grained divide than that seen during the Cold War. While I have been arguing that interdependence between China and the West has become a source of tension and less interdependence might bring some stability, no doubt this process will be costly and painful for ordinary citizens. I hope this book will help readers to make sense of how China and the West arrived where they are and provide the conceptual tools for imagining where the relationship is heading.

Writing a book is a lonely endeavour, yet one meets several people along the way. To begin with, this book was conceived thanks to my friendship with Dr Hannah Bretherton who was impact and engagement manager at the Lau China Institute. Not only was she a great support and helped me to connect with colleagues and events at the Lau – where I was an affiliate – but she also suggested to the publisher of this book that I might offer a valuable contribution to the debate on China. By the time I started the process to formally join the Lau China Institute in late summer 2022, she had left for a prestigious job as head of public diplomacy at the Australian High Commission – luckily, just next door. I wish her all the best.

Going back to early 2018, special thanks go to Dr Warren Chin, my colleague at the Defence Studies Department. As head of education, he allowed me to develop my first course on China. Teaching high-ranking military students from the UK and the rest of the world has been inspiring and it has provided me with a chance to gauge how different countries see China. As crucial to the development of my views on China and the world have been all those academic organizations, media outlets, colleagues and journalists that have given me the opportunity of expressing, and by doing so, shaping and enriching my views along the way. The list is too long to be unpacked here, and it stretches from Italy to the UK, from continental Europe to the Middle East, from India to China. Finally, I am grateful to those who have had a direct impact on this book and who made it possible. Stefanie Borkum, my professional proofreader, has patiently corrected this draft and its revised version, not to mention several other works of mine in recent years, from my first manuscript to many other short publications. If these works are in fluent English, it is thanks to her.

Professor Kerry Brown leads this series for Agenda Publishing. He has been sympathetic to this project since the beginning. Alison Howson, my editor at Agenda, has always been very supportive, from helping me handle challenging comments of peer reviewers to reading and editing the draft of this book. All remaining errors are my own.

Introduction

Diplomatic tensions between the People's Republic of China (PRC) and the United States (US) did not end when President Donald Trump, fervent advocate for a trade war with Beijing, left the White House in January 2021. On the contrary, tensions have continued into the first year of the Biden administration, through the first months of the Russian invasion of Ukraine and will likely last until the end of Biden's mandate. Indeed, if Trump made China into an almost personal issue for him and his inner circle of advisors, Biden, with a more institutionally sensitive style, has sought to bring the most important agencies of his administration under a coordinated effort. A resolute and comprehensive stance towards China has now become a long-term policy of the US. Likewise, on the other side of the Pacific Ocean Xi Jinping, communist party high officials and foreign minister Wang Yi demonstrated little intention of making any meaningful progress in US–China relations by accommodating some of the long-standing American requests. The fallout between American and Chinese top diplomats at a summit held in Anchorage (Alaska) in March 2021, weeks after Biden was sworn in, signalled that the relationship has a long way to go before any positive developments are seen. The drama of the Ukraine war, furthermore, made it unpalatable for many countries to maintain normal relations with Russia. This put China's relationship with Russia under the spotlight and encouraged the US, the European Union (EU), and G7 members to exert pressure on Beijing for picking a side, the message being: you are either with the West or with the war criminals of the Kremlin.

The frenzy that the word "China" tends to provoke in Washington was captured in an opinion piece in *The Atlantic* by former national security advisor Herbert R. McMaster published at the end of 2020, a tense year in US–China relations. He emphasized that there had been a sort of revelation moment about China, stating that assumptions in the rest of the world about China's modernization "were proving to be wrong" (McMaster 2020). To McMaster, China is a threat because it is governed by an authoritarian model that it exports abroad; meanwhile, the PRC bends the rules of the international order and exerts military influence over the South China Sea, Taiwan and the East China Sea. McMaster's view has been echoed across the West, although governments in Australia, the United Kingdom (UK), South Korea and the EU – to name a few – continue to maintain different degrees of strategic ambiguity in their China policy. In addition, relations with China have become a divisive factor throughout the West, not so much between states – although, the West is not that united when it comes to China – but within states, especially between different sections of society.

The fact that discontent about China has been spreading across the West since the second half of the 2010s confirms that each bilateral relationship with China cannot escape frictions which are structural rather than resulting from the whim of a particular leader – although, this is not to say that different administrations and government coalitions cannot have their own agenda about China. Policy-makers, journalists and citizens have been wondering what is happening between China and the West and why. As I sought to explain in a previous book, US foreign policy towards China since Obama's "pivot to Asia" has showed that the root causes of current frictions lie more in the sphere of the technological and geopolitical implications of the rise of an authoritarian China to the detriment of American hegemony (Leoni 2021). The dichotomy between liberal democracy and autocracy per se – used by McMaster and many others in the US – only provides a superficial, and very American, account of a more complex issue (Kroenig 2020).

The aim of this book is to help western fellow citizens reflect critically on the rise of China as a state whose power has increased extremely quickly over the past few decades; and whose system of government and values is far from that of western democracy. While public, political and academic debates in the West have been characterized by a frenzy about the PRC's relationship with the world in recent years, this book shows that China matters very much to the contemporary world order, and its geopolitical rise and institutional authoritarianism are not so out of the ordinary as many believe. However, the aim of this book is to encourage its readers to replace a frenzied attitude with a more sober, historically and theoretically informed view of the drivers and implications of China's rise. However, a critical and sober interpretation of the PRC's trajectory to international prominence does not imply blind acceptance of China's rise or of its implications. It is meant to lead to a more realistic China policy.

Western politicians and citizens would not be so concerned about China if the latter was a sealed-up state like North Korea, no matter its size. It is China's geoeconomic openness – although, not as much as some would like – and interdependence with the West that carries major implications. This leads to the academic backdrop of the book and the theme that underlies the different chapters. The relationship between China and the West must be contextualized in the liberal international order (LIO). While the LIO, from several points of view, has represented a major step forward in the history of humankind, it is the product of an irresolvable tension between the sovereign states that established and maintained it, and those free global interactions – be these economic, human or cybernetic – that the LIO itself was meant to promote. This conundrum has always existed both in the progenitors of the LIO and since its establishment after the Second World War. However, China's joining of this international club has come with structural consequences. Countries attempt to manage these, but all too often they do so in a diplomatically uncoordinated manner which, given the size and integration of China's economy into the global economy, is not effective. Indeed China, authoritarianism notwithstanding, has become a capitalist champion, and the West needs its consumerism for the global economy to prosper. It goes without saying that rejecting, containing, criticizing or fighting China implies challenging our own way of life. But as some of the chapters of this book shows, the West has failed for too long to take the bull by the horns.

A GLOBAL ECONOMY IN A WORLD OF SOVEREIGN STATES: THE CONUNDRUM OF THE LIO

The strict control of national borders that most states have implemented since the outbreak of Covid-19 has been a cold shower for those hyperglobalists whom, at the end of the Cold War, announced that the state as a political sovereign institution was withering. Restrictions put in place against the spread of the pandemic, instead, were a stark reminder that states are still in charge within their sovereign territory and in international relations. The example will sound banal to most observers, yet reveals a great deal. The imposition of two or three weeks of hotel quarantine for travellers entering Australia, Thailand or the UK – with fines of around £5,000 for those seeking to leave Britain to go on a holiday – weighs heavily on those who believed that institutions of global governance had eroded the primacy of the state.

The global pandemic, however, is only the latest friction in the problematic relationship between sovereign states and a global economy made of flows and networks of trade of goods, trafficking of human beings, legal and illegal migration, transnational terrorism, transnational backlashes of financial crises and environmental problems, among many other things. This friction has been a constant as states – fixed in space – and capitalism – with its tendency to transgress political barriers – coexist. The LIO, as pointed out above, encapsulates this tension. It is an institutional infrastructure formed by national pluralist democracies but characterized by a thrust towards global governance that challenges the Westphalian system of states. After the Peace of Westphalia in 1648, "no single claim to truth or universal rule had prevailed in Europe's contests" and each state "would acknowledge the domestic structures and religious vocations of its fellow states as realities and refrain from challenging their existence" (Kissinger 2011: 3). The LIO, instead, has to an extent sought to overcome this structure by creating universal values and interests, a hard enterprise in such a diverse and fragmented world order.

But the world order is still far from becoming state-less, although the global economy continues to have a major impact on our everyday lives. For the time being the LIO remains a strange, Janus-faced beast where at its heart lies the irreconcilable tension between national political interests and transnational economic interests.

Student and advocate of the LIO, John J. Ikenberry captured this tension by acknowledging that this order is made of both "liberal states and liberal order building"; that within it, different formations and arrangements can materialize, and there can be many kinds of LIO; and that the LIO "can affirm and embody principles of state sovereignty and national self-determination or champion more supranational forms of shared sovereignty" (Ikenberry 2011: 18–20). This shows that even to those who have an ideological attraction to it, the LIO is a contradictory composite of many values and interests and, in this sense, it reflects the diversity and the flaws of the idea of the West. Indeed, scholars who are more critical of the LIO have articulated further the sources of this tension and unveiled the fact that there can be, within the same countries, competing interests between different groups of elites. To the geographer David Harvey there are "two logics", one is that of the businessperson who operates across states to expand markets and reach as many consumers as possible worldwide; the other is that of national political elites, whose power and work is fixed, that is, limited to the territory of the state they rule (Harvey 2003: 27–30). This relationship is often the source of disagreements between the most influential individuals and groups of a country. As the sociologist Manuel Castells explained, the businessperson seeks to "escape" political restrictions, unless these are meant to protect his or her business; meanwhile, political leaders have to guard the state from external threats and cannot – or should not – think in the interest of this or that entrepreneur, rather they have to find a compromise for the sake of national interests (Castells 2010: 446).

This tension, as different parts of this book demonstrate, is crucial to explaining the origins of many quarrels between the US or western countries and China. To complicate this picture, states are not purely independent actors, but they generally abide to a set of international rules of diplomacy, trade, human rights, and so on, that define the prevailing order. International rules and regimes are never neutral, a fact that clearly China has understood through its relationship with the US. Indeed, while the above-described dichotomy is a real problem in policy-making, one must not forget that economic flows normally circulate according to sets of rules established by states which have been "active agents" in determining how exchanges between one another should be conducted; influential states or more commonly "great powers" have the upper hand in the determination of these rules. Doing so allows powerful states to manipulate the security-economy conundrum in their favour. As the geopolitical intellectual Colin Flint put it, political power is more than "controlling territory, it is also a matter of controlling movement" but it is also about the ability and strength of "being able to construct networks to one's own advantage across political boundaries" (Flint 2017: 179) One of the pillars of Pax Americana – that is, US hegemony – has been exactly that of convincing other states through both persuasion and coercion to accept rules, such as the free-market rule of law, that were favourable to Washington (Leoni 2021: 64–77). In essence "leading states, operating within this system of states, … have pursued liberal order building" following geopolitical logics (Ikenberry 2011: 21). As briefly discussed in the book, China wants to reform these rules that have up to now favoured developed countries. The US is desperately trying to protect current rules as a way of maintaining its geopolitical primacy.

The relationship between security and economic interests, however, is not a permanent state of affairs in the international system; adjustments can take place with the break-up of crises and systemic changes in the international system. During the Cold War, for instance, concerns of foreign policy-makers and defence planning were strong enough to trump business interests for the sake of security, because the Atlantic bloc faced what it believed to be an existential threat. The "iron curtain", the war in Vietnam and Korea, the embargo on Cuba and a developed welfare state also aimed at containing Soviet ideological influence in countries like Italy and the Federal Republic of Germany; these measures, restricted the space for private enterprise. On the contrary, the end of the Cold War led to the (false) belief that power politics and geopolitical competition were over, that the expansion of the LIO through what we know as neoliberal globalization was the new mantra that had to prevail over strategic interests. Thirty years after the fall of the Berlin Wall, the deep impact of China's engagement with the world economy, in addition to Covid-19, have been a wake-up call for rebalancing the relationship between economic and security interests after the radical, hyperglobalist turn of the post-Cold War years.

STRUCTURE AND ARGUMENTS OF THE BOOK

Building on the provocative intellectual assumption that the ascent of a non-democratic great power like China is not, from a historical viewpoint, out of the ordinary, this book endeavours to answer several related questions. Chapters 1–4 provide a picture of Sino-western relations and China's growing engagement with the world that emphasizes nuances rather than making black-and-white claims. Meanwhile, Chapter 5 contains an update on contemporary issues in Sino-western relations.

Chapters 1 and 2 develop the most contentious claims in this book. Chapter 1 seeks to make sense of two important aspects in the relationship between China and the West, such as the PRC's hybrid socio-institutional system and the regional geopolitical and global geoeconomic rise of China. It is argued that while these events challenge Euro- or western-centrism, these are not so unusual in history. Due to the uneven development of capitalism, the geopolitical balance of power will fluctuate over the decades and centuries, which means that we should never take any status quo for granted for too long. However, China's state capitalism and more broadly the merging of free-market economy into a Confucian context through communist – and formerly imperial – structures – are not alien to the world we live in; liberal democracies and the LIO are just one model of society among several and they must coexist with competing models – especially in Asia, where most of the world's population lives.

The second claim of the book – in Chapter 2 – is about the role that the West has played in the PRC's success story. Indeed, the West has actively engaged China for centuries; most importantly, it has pursued and provoked – and to an extent it continues to do so – the opening of China to the world and its rise. By taking a longer perspective on Sino-western and, especially, Sino-American relations, one can see that events of the last decade are the result not only of longer historical trends but also of patterns of political decisions that governments – such as US administrations – have consistently pursued. Simply put, the PRC nowadays has become what the West – especially Britain and the US – has always wanted from China; although it has not become exactly what the West wished. Even when some alarming signals – for instance, during the tragic events of Tiananmen Square and in the rest of China in 1991, just to cite one instance – were evident, the West autonomously decided to hold its nose and continue business as usual with China. Not doing so, as explained above, would have impacted on the western way of life.

The third issue that this book seeks to address, in Chapters 3 and 4, is the fact that there is a patchier picture in China's relationship with the West than is often portrayed by the media.

Progressively, from Chapter 3 to Chapter 4, the book shows that while the US and the West bear great responsibility for setting in motion the success of the PRC, China's ascent in the world is not as victorious as is often portrayed. China's attempt at catching up quickly with the West and its integration into the LIO not only causes dilemmas for the West, but also for China itself.

In Chapter 3, the book reflects on the success of China at the international level and in the West. Until a few years ago China was not a subject of discussion outside of some scholarly and diplomatic circles. Today, instead, it hits the headlines of newspapers and television news. This sudden rise to prominence of China among western civil society makes this process look more dramatic, taking place at a speed that national politicians and those tasked with the security of countries cannot control. The media headlines tend to portray China's rise and foreign policy achievements in the world as a mark of its success and as the result of a carefully calculated strategy. Yet, while China has become a great power in some ways, it continues to display vulnerabilities which will take years to address. While its foreign investments tend to attract a lot of attention, China is not "taking over" every realm of social life.

Chapter 4, along similar lines, reflects on the extent to which China – now an active participant to the LIO – also faces dramatic dilemmas not different in nature from those the West is dealing with in its relationship with Beijing. This shows that the LIO is a source of tension for China also, and not only for western capitalist democracies. How is China managing the conundrums posed by the LIO? If the West has woken up three decades after the end of the Cold War realizing that for too long economic aspirations have trumped strategic interests, China is facing the opposite problem: it must increase its engagement with the outside world but it does not want to give up its domestic, authoritarian political structure and its aspirations for geopolitical leadership. Can China continue to succeed without decentralizing political power? A possible response to this is a trend towards decoupling currently underway.

The final chapter takes the reader back to the starting point of the book, that is, to recent events and tensions between China and influential western states, and seeks to bring to life the China-conundrum by focusing on the uncertainty faced by some western countries when dealing with Beijing. By looking at a few important case studies, the chapter argues that current Sino-western relations have entered a new phase compared to the post-Cold War years. However, the West remains not only a very ambiguous concept but also a fragile geopolitical construct. Indeed, it is shown that the West is not a united geopolitical bloc when it comes to China – in contrast to the Cold War years – as confirmed during the 2021 G7 Summit in the UK. While ideologically and militarily western countries have manifested substantial concerns, China continues to charm them with the economic opportunities its huge market provides. This dilemma has led to a degree of ambiguity in the China policy of countries like the US, the UK, Germany, Israel, South Korea, Australia, Italy and many others.

In this regard, if there are a few reasons to argue that we are slowly entering a post-western era – in addition to a post-American one – this is also because of the rise of China, although one should broaden this to the rise of Asia with its competing values and institutional models. Nonetheless, the war in Ukraine and China's support for Russia has given the West one more reason to stick to this loose concept, accelerating a trend towards decoupling. Yet, it is important to reflect on whether recent developments in western countries' policy towards China – such as the end of the "golden era" in the UK and the "reality check" in Australia – are manifestations of radical policy shifts or mere tactical adjustments. Although this book advocates for states to employ a sober and realistic policy towards China, clearly too many western countries expound an incoherent China policy.

China's rise and state capitalism:
an uneven world order

> "There is no force whatsoever that can substitute for the People's Republic of China represented by the Communist Party of China. This is not an empty word. It is something which has been proven and tested over several decades of experience".
>
> Deng Xiaoping, 1989

In the first years of the twentieth century, the passage of hegemonic power from British to American world leadership did not lead to a direct confrontation between the declining and the rising great powers. Historians of international relations are still debating why this is the case: because of cultural similarity and shared historical experience; or because London saw Washington as a lesser evil compared to Germany, Japan and the USSR; or because the competition within the Anglo-American sphere of influence was economic rather than military (Hugill 2009).

There were important reasons for the two great powers not to fight one another. Competition and mistrust also characterized this relationship, but for Washington and London it was easier to overcome the contradictions caused by the liberal international order (LIO). Managing a power transition, however, is more challenging when it comes to Sino-western relations in today's globalized world.

The intersection between capitalism and an international system of states is the backdrop to two important historical processes which are fundamental to understanding why China poses a challenge to the West. In particular, this chapter deals with the combination between western capitalism and national political systems that are not capitalist or pre-date capitalism and that have contributed to socio-political hybridity in the international system; it also seeks to make sense of the geoeconomic unevenness caused by a globalized capitalist order which is the source of great powers' rise and fall.

Two main points emerge from this discussion. First, China's hybridity is not a unique phenomenon but has to be contextualized in a world order and a region – Asia – which is diverse and where democracy has not put down solid roots, as many liberal thinkers had hoped. Second, the rise of the People's Republic of China (PRC) confirms patterns that have characterized the ascent of other capitalist states, albeit with certain Chinese peculiarities and on a remarkable scale.

BEYOND WESTERN-CENTRISM: A DIVERSE WORLD ORDER

In his book *World Order*, Henry Kissinger, former US National Security Advisor (NSA) to President Richard Nixon, criticized the concept of "international community"; he noted that this term is "invoked perhaps more insistently now than in any other era", but there are still too many parts of the world for which this concept does not represent a "clear or agreed set of goals" (Kissinger 2014: 2). A key message from this is that western-centrism and the exceptionalism of western principles – be they good or bad – tend to be blind to an international environment characterized by social, cultural and institutional diversity.

The idea of "international community" as a pillar of the western world order is at odds with two truths: first, that there is an "outside" to the West, that is, the western order or the LIO does not encompass every corner of the globe. The rise of Asia, and more specifically China, serves as a reminder that such diversity continues to govern the life of a large portion of international society. Second, and following from the previous point – regions outside the West "have played a minimal role" in establishing the foundational rules of the LIO and nowadays tend to "question their validity" (*ibid.*). With his pragmatic worldview, Kissinger pointed out that "[n]o truly global 'world order' has ever existed" and "[o]ur age is insistently, at times almost desperately, in pursuit of a concept of world order" (*ibid.*).

The problem for Kissinger is that when attempting to establish a dominant world order, inclusiveness is key to success because for one order to dominate it has to incorporate all other orders (*ibid.*: 8–9). Kissinger sees in modern history the existence of four different orders: the European or Westphalian one, China's *tianxia* order, the religion-led Islamic order, and the idealist order of the United States. However, the European order through imperial wars has managed to successfully spread to other regions and contaminate them with its political and economic ideas. But as the theory of "uneven and combined development" of capitalism (U&CD) maintains, this has been an uneven endeavour, in the sense that the European, and later, western order has had to coexist with competing institutional, economic and value systems. Over the years, with the spread of capitalism to Latin America, Asia, eastern Europe and Africa, this encounter has been the engine of much social and "political multiplicity" as several countries have managed to adopt western capitalism while maintaining indigenous and even ancient political institutions (Rolf 2021: 23–4).

The coexistence of different societal models in one state or region, however, is not the product of an accident of history. Developed countries, especially Britain and the United States, in the twentieth and twenty-first century, exported capitalism to expand the global economic space and maximize profits. Meanwhile, developing countries have sought to incorporate western developmental prescriptions to catch up and overcome domestic weaknesses (Allinson & Anievas 2009: 50–51). On this point, U&CD theory suggests that undeveloped or developing countries seeking to escape both economic poverty and geopolitical inferiority may act based on the "whip of external necessity", that is, external economic and geopolitical pressures from more developed countries; in this way they seek to break away from their condition by leveraging what Trotsky called "the privilege of historic backwardness" and "skipping a whole series of intermediate stages" (Trotsky 2008: 4–5). They can leapfrog and catch up with advanced capitalist economies by following a fast-paced path to industrialization. However, development takes place with such speed and unevenness that it does not always sweep away pre-capitalist cultural, social and institutional features; rather, what takes place is a process of combination, that is, the formation of a hybrid reality where elements of western capitalism coexist with different cultures and social relations. The product is a unique, "peculiar" nation-based type of capitalism – as in the case of the PRC (Rolf 2021: 26).

This variegated picture and its implications are all too often neglected by western policy-makers, who tend to stigmatize diversity. Assuming that there is socio-political homogeneity within the group of western nations – where in fact, many differences and disagreements on substantial issues remain – world states continue to operate internally according to distinct systems, and this also has an impact on international politics. If China – the subject of this book – remains the most striking example of combined development, it is by no means an exception. While it seems easy to point to the fact that more than half of African states are non-electoral democracies – many of which resemble dictatorships – one has also to consider Asia. With 60 per cent of the world population – the most inhabited continent – it seems impossible to speculate about world order without including it in the analysis.

A recent study on the state of democracy in Asia by the Brookings Institution – an American think tank – confirmed that while Asia is home to some of the most populous democracies, its "relationship with democratic governance is admittedly complicated" (Ford & Hass 2021). The report concluded that aside from Thailand, the Philippines, Myanmar and Sri Lanka – countries where freedom has been eroded – support for democracy remains high. Yet, "some of the greatest dissatisfaction with democratic performance occurs in the region's more consolidated democracies: Japan and South Korea" (*ibid.*). While in these two countries there is support for freedom and transparency, "the importance they attach to specific democratic ideals" is weaker than in Europe or the United States. Given the influence of Confucianism and other traditions, democratic values in Asia compete with interests such as "stability", a condition that often can undermine healthy competition between political parties. For instance, Japan together with South Korea are the most westernized of all Asian countries; Japan has been on the side of the United States in diplomatic matters since the end of the Second World War; and it is a member of the G7, the leading forum of western democracies. Yet, if one considers the period between 1955 and 2021 – 66 years – Japan has been ruled by the same party for a total of 60 years. Alternation between parties in government should be one of the pillars of pluralist democracies, but this is clearly not the case in this part of the world.

Western expectations about "a general shift to more democracy in the [so-called] 'second' modernity, are unfulfilled" in Asia, a researcher argued (Schmidt 2016: 13). Since the early 1990s, academics working in the field of democracy and government studies, including Francis Fukuyama, have maintained that the Asian way of government resembles a sort of "soft authoritarianism" (Roy 1994: 231–41). This concept captures two features of Asian political systems. On the one hand, it refers to the combination between market-oriented economy with paternalistic relationship between rulers and ruled. On the other hand, it champions "communitarian" values and "conformity to group interests over individual rights". This is, to give another example, the case of Singapore (*ibid.*). As Fukuyama put it in a paper on Confucianism and democracy, Asian citizens regard the latter with scepticism. However, this is not because they reject the principle of democracy itself. Rather, it is because of the perception that it does not result in "reconciling individual rights with the interests of the larger community", which they see as the cause of moral decay in western policy-making (Fukuyama 1995).

This discussion of Asian government is important for two reasons. On the one hand, it gives us a sense of the context within which China has existed and from which it has emerged. On the other hand, it helps us understand the cultural and socio-institutional fundamentals of the Chinese form of government. While the Chinese type of authoritarianism is not a "soft" one, the Asian context helps make sense of what interests might drive this model compared to western ones. If this is the case, idealism of the American neo-conservative kind and strategies aimed at exporting democracy risk being based on unrealistic, flawed analyses, and ultimately will frustrate hopes for change. In his book on Sino-American relations, Kishore Mahbubani, former Singaporean ambassador to the United Nations noted that "[w]hen it comes to analysing political systems, American analysts tend to veer toward a black-and-white view of the world: open or closed society, democratic or totalitarian society, liberal or authoritarian" (Mahbubani 2020: 164). He asked why Americans "assume" that engagement with China will one day lead to democratization. The answer he gave is that Americans – like many western pundits and politicians – "believe that [liberal] democracies stand on the right side of history", a claim "strongly reinforced" by the end of the Soviet Union in 1989 and Fukuyama's slogan, popular within policy circles, the "end of history" (*ibid.*: 135).

UNEVEN DEVELOPMENT: THE RISE AND FALL OF GREAT POWERS

The West has been afflicted by western-centrism. One of the manifestations of this misjudgement is the unspoken but palpable perception that the West has always been successful, that this success is guaranteed for eternity, and that it can spread its wealth to the rest of the world. In parallel to this, classical economics has posited for years that one day there will be an equalization of the global economic space and all citizens and states of the world will be able to enjoy the same – high – standard of living. Unfortunately, this process is patchier than what "hyper-globalist" scholars have argued – it is more a zero-sum situation than a win-win one. If Chinese people get richer, European or American citizens will get poorer. Indeed, American sociologist and economic historian Immanuel Wallerstein explained that "states [can] change their position in the world-economy, from semiperiphery to core, and vice versa", however, "all states cannot 'develop' simultaneously by definition, since the system functions by virtue of having unequal core and peripheral regions" (Wallerstein 1979: 61). With the theory of "uneven development" (UD) of capitalism it is easier to understand how ephemeral the West's primacy and wealth could be. The capitalist world economy is anything but static, and with every successive decade it moves faster than ever with its highly volatile geoeconomic patterns (Leoni 2021: 94).

More importantly for this book, UD is the driver of major shifts in economic and military relations of power between core states and those of the semi-periphery and periphery of the international system – once known by the derogatory terms "Second" and "Third World". In 1987, British historian of international relations Paul Kennedy published his magnum opus, *The Rise and Fall of the Great Powers*. His argument was built on the assumption that in an international system each state strives "to enhance its wealth and its power"; therefore, "[t]he relative strengths of the leading nations in world affairs never remain constant" due to two main factors, "the uneven rate of growth" between states and the benefit from sudden "technological and organizational breakthroughs" (*ibid.*: xv–vi). Indeed, in his book, each of the eight chapters provides insights in different ways into how the geopolitical balance of power has changed eight times between 1500 and 2000.

These arguments found a more sophisticated theoretical grounding in a pamphlet written about 70 years before Kennedy's bestseller by the Russian revolutionary Vladimir Ilyich Lenin. He maintained that due to the tendency of the rate of profit to fall in developed countries, businesses looked for new, more generous opportunities for investment abroad. According to Lenin, "surpluses" were reinvested in "backward countries [where] profits are usually high, for capital is scarce, the price of land is relatively low, wages are low, raw materials are cheap" (Lenin 1939: 63). These investments can trigger – although not always, as the underdevelopment of Africa demonstrates – the economic ascent of countries. In a famous passage from *Imperialism, the Highest Stage of Capitalism* written during the First World War, Lenin stated that "Half a century ago, Germany was a miserable, insignificant country, as far as its capitalist strength was concerned, compared with the strength of England at that time. Japan was similarly insignificant compared with Russia. Is it 'conceivable' that in ten or twenty years' time the relative strength of the imperialist powers will have remained unchanged?" (*ibid.*: 118–9). Absolutely inconceivable.

These shifts are also a source of tension between rival states that do not want to see their status and economic privileges decline. For now, however, the main point is that the economic centre of gravity in recent decades has been moving at a greater speed than ever before and away from Europe. This has happened because of the inception of capitalism and technology in industrializing and developing countries, particularly in the global South, where a great amount of cheap labour was available compared to in Europe or the US. Asia has been the true winner in this core–periphery competitive dynamic. Commenting on a 2012 report on the shifting economic centre of gravity, *The Economist* stated that "it is striking how fast this seems to be happening", at a speed of 140 kilometres per year (The Economist 2012). About a decade later, a McKinsey report noted that while Asia in 2000 "accounted for just under one-third of global GDP (in PPP terms)", it is currently "on track to top 50 percent by 2040", and to "account for 40 percent of the world's total consumption" (Tonby *et al.* 2019: 3).

Today, scholars agree that "the world order is in a transition", and that it has been so for more than ten years (Leoni 2021: 91). "Transition" really means that relations of power between states are changing; states that used to be rich, mighty and influential have seen their power declining as weaker but rising powers have caught up. Until the start of the Second World War, for instance, Britain was the leading great power, although a declining one. Since the end of the war, the United States has been displacing the UK from the throne; by the early twenty-first century the US was described as a quasi-global hegemon. After the turn of the century, however, China's economic power has been closing the gap with the US while its military power has continued to grow – although at a slower pace. While the EU and the former colonial powers like Britain, France, Belgium, Germany and Italy have experienced a time of financial austerity, Asia as a whole has been in a state of economic and technological ferment – with some exceptions, like Japan. Overall, in the past few decades there has been a draining of wealth from the West by the East. In a period of only 20 years – that is, between the end of the Cold War in 1989 and the Great Recession in 2008 – the world order has shifted from a US-led unipolar system to a phase of transition. The future world order will probably be multipolar, with power shared by three or more dominant states that can balance one another; although some observers worry that it might even be "apolar", that is, without recognized leaders and, therefore, chaotic. While there are no certainties, many agree that the new world order will be neither unipolar nor led by the US. As the power of the US was global in aspiration, but never really capable of imposing its will in every corner of the world, regions will have new "spoilers" if not local hegemons; for the first time in many years, the so-called "resurgence" of Russia and the consolidation of Chinese power in the western Pacific region might prevent any external competitor from taking the lead (*ibid.*: 97–102).

Meanwhile, the emergence of heavyweights like China and Russia is not the only challenge to the unipolar order. The spread of new technologies and investments of states in niche capabilities allows even small and medium powers to play a role. Rory Medcalf, head of the National Security College (NSC) at the Australian National University, noted how

Japan, India, Indonesia and Australia – but one could also add South Korea – by 2050 "are expected to have a combined population of 2.108 billion and a combined GDP (PPP) of an astounding US$63.97 trillion", against the "379 million people and a GDP (PPP) of US$34 trillion of the United States. Meanwhile, their defense budget combined could be 'larger' than that of the People's Liberation Army" (Medcalf 2019: 61–2).

As the writer Parag Khanna pointed out, we are past the point when a western resurgence could "blunt Asia's resurrection" because "Asia's rise is structural, not cyclical", as this section of the book has sought to show (Khanna 2019: 20). Although ideas and hopes about the decline of Asia abound, Khanna wrote, "Asianization of the world", like the Europeanization of the world in previous centuries, cannot be stopped (*ibid.*: 20–24).

CHINA'S RISE

We can conclude from the previous section that power in the international system will be much more shared. Richard Dobbs, who, among others, researched the shifting economic centre of gravity, noted that the "main reason" for the global shift in relations of wealth is China's rise (*The Economist* 2012). Most will agree that the PRC's race to catch up from the late 1970s to today has been impressive, but this can be better appreciated from a historical perspective. Until Britain's industrial revolution in the late eighteenth century, China was the biggest economy in the world. At the time, productivity per worker was roughly the same everywhere, and China with its huge population scored high. Living standards between China and the West were similar. Furthermore, the Chinese had for centuries been at the forefront of technological discoveries, while Europe "was just catching up ... and still unable to manufacture cotton, silks, or porcelains as fine as those produced in India and China" (Goldstone 2008: 166–7).

Between the eighteenth and nineteenth century, however, Europe overtook Asia in what became known as the "Great Divergence", as historian Kenneth Pomeranz called it (2000). The reasons for Europe overtaking Asia are debated among academics, but the answer will probably have to take into account different factors, such as technological, cultural and geopolitical ones. On the one hand, the industrial revolution in Britain was facilitated by easy access to coal whereas China's coal reserves were deep in the mainland; meanwhile, British society experienced the diffusion of a "Baconian spirit" in its approach to science, and a change in the relationship between religion and secularism. On the other hand, Britain, Japan, Portugal, the United States and others invested their power granted by technological progress in imperialist adventures, which held back the freedom and progress of China – in addition to that of many other countries – through the Opium Wars – discussed in the next chapter. By the time the "Century of Humiliation" was almost over, at the end of the Second World War, China "had become the world's poorest country" (Arrighi 2007: 4).

Mahbubani stated that because China and India were "the two largest economies" until 1820, China's comeback in the late twentieth century represents the end of an "aberration" (Mahbubani 2020: 71). Similarly, Australian strategist Hugh White observed that the rise of China "is less a revolution than a restoration – a return to normal after a two-century interlude" (White 2013: 30). Aside from the provocative flavour of these arguments, both Mahbubani and White emphasized a tendency within world orders to shift balance of economic and, consequently, military power, but in recent decades such shifts – as in the case of China – have happened at a greater speed. Indeed, the reasons for China's impressive recovery are not to be found in some drive for vengeance, as both authors pointed out, although the Chinese elite have been agent of change and have often attached a revanchist tone to their narratives. Instead, one must look at the opening up of the PRC to a world capitalist economy, and to the inflow of foreign investments, technology and skills that enabled it to leverage on a huge amount of low-cost labour. In a way, the PRC could never have achieved such miraculous economic growth if it were not for Mao's "[d]isastrous" policies (Rolf 2021: 97). China was the periphery that European and American imperialism had long waited to find, and it had a potential for investments that developed economies could not offer.

There have been different waves in this relentless ascent of China from an undeveloped country to a great power, such as the first chunk of reforms in the 1980s, the post-Tiananmen years of the 1990s, and the 2000s when China joined the World Trade Organisation (WTO). The

Third Plenary Session of the 11th Central Committee of the Chinese Communist Party in December 1978 was a historical watershed of paramount importance. It announced an open-door policy aimed at engaging in economic cooperation and adopting foreign technology under the "Law of the People's Republic of China on Joint Venture Using Chinese and Foreign Investment" (Tzeng 1991: 270–1). Deng Xiaoping stated that "we should allow some regions, some enterprises, some workers and farmers, ... to be better rewarded and improve on their livelihood". One year later cities like Shenzhen, Zhuhai and Shantou together with Xiamen in Fujian became special economic zones (SEZs). The aim was to "attract and absorb foreign technology and capital to contribute to a self-reliant national construction" (*ibid.*); the SEZs allowed China to do this and to enter global production chains of manufactured goods, seizing markets with its export-driven model (Yeung *et al.* 2009: 236), at a time when "globalization was gathering momentum" in the early 1980s. Shenzhen was the most remarkable success experiment of all as it turned from being a *tabula rasa*, that is, a "small fishing village of 30,000 population encompassing no more than 3 km² of dilapidated buildings, lacking even a traffic light" to a Chinese Silicon Valley (*ibid.*: 223). This process had spill-over effects into the countryside.

The second period unfolded in the post-Tiananmen Square years during which liberalization and privatization accelerated. In his southern tour, Deng sought to put China's agenda of reform back on track and to strengthen the image of the CCP under the slogan "development is the absolute principle". The 14th Party Congress in October 1992 approved additional measures to encourage foreign trade, raise growth targets, and above all, to allow greater development in the private sector that pushed the PRC towards a "socialist market economy" – a phrase which until 1978 was an ideological oxymoron. Paternalistic frameworks – such as corporate benefits and the *danwei* system more broadly – were dismantled, while discussions about entering the General Agreement on Tariffs and Trade (GATT) were ongoing from the late 1980s (Rolf 2021: 104). In the mid- to late-1990s, the vast majority of state-owned enterprises were effectively privatized and the number dropped dramatically in the early 2000s. Dealing with a "balance of payments crisis" in 1993, the renminbi was devalued from US\$5.76 to US\$8.62 while tax rebates were offered to export industries (*ibid.*: 106–7).

This however was not enough to make the Chinese economy fly. The benefits of capitalist development can quickly run out of steam and – as the imperialist foreign policies of the West have shown – the government is tasked with creating constant opportunities, from delivering trade agreements to conquering new markets and territories. As China joined a capitalist mode of production it was drawn into its contradictions as well; it was compelled to embark on the necessary exponential growth imposed on countries by this economic model. This led the communist leadership to look more ambitiously at the global economy and in particular to the WTO. To do so, China had to "relax over 7,000 tariffs, quotas and other trade barriers" in total (*The Economist* 2011a). This was a "successful" move as "contracted foreign direct investment quadrupled from 1999–2005 to $160bn a year" and "GDP growth trended sharply upwards over the following 7 years, hitting 14% in 2007–2008" (Rolf 2021: 113). On the tenth anniversary of the PRC membership of the WTO, *The Economist* concluded that "the bet paid off for China. It has blossomed into the world's greatest exporter and second-biggest importer. The marriage of foreign know-how, Chinese labour and the open, global market has succeeded beyond anyone's predictions" (*The Economist* 2011c).

Overall, China's GDP grew from $149.541 billion in 1978 to $1.211 trillion between 1978 and 2000, and from $1.211 trillion to $14.28 trillion in the first two decades of this century (World Bank data 2020). This meant that from 1979 to 2018, China's annual real GDP averaged 9.5 per cent while Beijing managed to "double the size of its economy in real terms every eight years" (Morrison 2019: 5). China, therefore, like other developing countries has managed to close the "gap in productivity" since capitalist practices and technologies have been incorporated into a demographically bigger territory (White 2013: 30). This has also paid off militarily since expenditure grew by more than ten times between the late 1990s and 2020, while US expenditure only doubled (World Bank).

As the PRC turned into a recipient of foreign direct investments, and it reorganized its economy to become an export-led powerhouse, the United States was becoming increasingly dependent on foreign production, meaning that its earnings were declining compared to its expenditure. This was the backlash of globalization. Globalization was meant to increase the profits of American corporations "by lowering production costs of imported goods and putting downward pressure on U.S. wages" (Palley 2012: 3–5), but it also allowed China to reach the sort of growth described above. Indeed, "[i]n 1980 non-petroleum imported goods were equal to 30.5 percent of US manufacturing GDP. By 2000, this ratio had risen to 78 percent; by 2007 it was 96.3 percent" and China was a fundamental source of these imports (*ibid.*). This picture could also be applied to other western countries. Such development led a *Forbes* commentator to write that "the Chinese have more money than God" thanks to their world's largest investment potential (Rapoza 2017). Hugh White was right in paraphrasing Pomeranz and in noting that about two centuries after the "Great Divergence" we are currently in the middle of a "Great Convergence" which, in a few years could mean China taking over (White 2013: 30).

The summer of 2008 was, in this regard, a moment of revelation. While the PRC's lavish opening ceremony at the Olympic Games in Beijing on 8 August showed the world the "glorious civilization" that China has been for several millennia, a few weeks later – on 15 September – the American bank Lehman Brothers crashed, unleashing a profound financial crisis from which the West has yet to fully recover. The ensuing Great Recession, as economists call it, wiped out $648 billion between early October 2008 and the end of December 2009, equivalent to an average of "$5,800 in lost income for each of the roughly 111 million U.S. households" (Swagel 2010). The first Obama administration had to intervene with a Marshall Plan for the twenty-first century. The Recovery and Reinvestment Act, with its massive injection of $800 billion, was the largest peacetime economic expansion programme in the country's history – at least until the Covid-19 pandemic. Although every single job taken away by the crisis was recovered, by the end of the Obama administration there were more low-paid jobs and less high- and medium-paid jobs compared to the pre-crisis years. American society became poorer.

Meanwhile, Beijing has not shied away from emphasizing how powerful it has become: when meeting Donald Trump, Xi Jinping commented none too subtly "[h]ow time flies. Over the past 45 years, historic changes have taken place in the world, in China, and in China–U.S. relations. ... The world today is experiencing tremendous progress, profound transformation, and major adjustments" (Xi & Trump 2017). This was Xi's call to end US unipolarity; there did not appear to be much the United States could do. The *Financial Times* wrote that during the years of the global financial crisis, western countries – especially the United States – sought, through multilateral regimes, to start "sharing power" albeit "on their terms" to constrain rising peer competitors within the framework of "responsible stakeholders in the global system" (Stephens 2008). But if there is one "big lesson" to be learnt from the crisis it is "that the west can no longer assume the global order will be remade in its own image" (*ibid.*).

CHINA'S HYBRIDITY AND THE CENTRALITY OF POLITICAL POWER

In the summer of 2021 as the last American troops remaining in Afghanistan were leaving the country, Taliban forces quickly retook control of the main cities including Kabul and established the Islamic Emirate of Afghanistan. This took place about 20 years after the US-led coalition had invaded the country with the aim of exporting democracy. This endeavour not only cost the US almost $1 trillion. In total, it led to the death of 2,448 US service members, 3,846 US contractors, 1,144 allied service members, 66,000 Afghan national military and police members, 47,245 civilians, 51,191 Taliban, 444 aid workers, and 72 journalists (Knickmeyer 2021). Whether or not violence is an efficient way of exporting democracy is not the point here. What is of greater interest to this book is that the quagmire of Afghanistan has put under the spotlight the limits of the West's one-size-fits-all foreign policy and democracy promotion agenda.

If the race of the PRC to become second world's economy has amazed many in the West, it is the resilience of its authoritarian political system that continues to puzzle politicians and analysts. This is for two reasons. First, authoritarianism is anathema to democratic societies. This has always been the case, even more so since the USSR's collapse and Fukuyama's call for the "end of history"; at that time, the mainstream mantra was that democracy achieved a final victory over competing political models. Second, the West is puzzled by China's political model because for a long time many believed that the PRC would have reformed its domestic institutions along with economic liberalization. Indeed, Trump's National Security Advisor McMaster has recalled how since the start of Deng Xiaoping's reforms, "the assumptions" were that having been welcomed into the international community, China would democratize (McMaster 2021). This expectation has informed US and western policies towards China in recent decades and continues to do so today – although several western governments have now realized that this will not happen any time soon.

But if people like McMaster and former secretary of state Mike Pompeo are quick to denounce the authoritarian form of government of the PRC, or to overemphasize the negative implications of communism, it is a problem because additional layers of complexity are overlooked. An aspect that deserves more attention in this regard is the relationship between the three Cs, that is, Confucianism, communism, and capitalism. Understanding this relationship allows us to make sense of the balance between openness and authoritarianism that we have seen in China in recent years. One must appreciate what the backbone of PRC's government is, why it is so durable, and why China has been enthusiastic about economic change and dynamism and yet so unreceptive to political change.

China has been ruled by an imperial system and through Confucian principles for 2,000 years. Key to understanding Confucianism is the context of Chinese history in which Confucius lived. His worldview "did not emerge from thin air": he witnessed the Warring States period – not too dissimilar from the popular television series *Game of Thrones* – an era of disorder which informed his views on good government. In his mind, a country needed to be based on a collectivist social contract, where ideas of "mutual obligation, maintenance of hierarchy, a belief in self-development, education, and improvement, and above all, an ordered society" figured prominently (Mitter 2016: 7–8). While Confucianism's popularity has had ups and downs in Chinese history, it has been an incredibly resistant cultural backdrop which continues to shape the way other political traditions have been integrated into China. Some features have been extremely resilient, partly to tackle external pressures and threats – whether represented by foreign invaders or globalization, as the next chapter explains. This continuity was not simply a convenience, nor was it an accident of history. Rather, it speaks to the resilience of Chinese culture even when violently suppressed by foreign invaders as during the Century of Humiliation. As Kissinger put it, for millennia, throughout the worst moment of Chinese modern history, "[t]he fundamental precepts of Chinese culture endured, tested by the strain of periodic calamity" (Kissinger 2011: 7). What the West overlooked with its one-size-fits-all policy of exporting democracy is that "[a]fter each collapse, the Chinese state reconstituted itself as if by some immutable law of nature" (*ibid.*).

The coexistence of Confucianism and communism is not so surprising. Historian Wang Gungwu argued that the PRC's communist state represents "a replacement for the old emperor-state", and that "Mao Zedong effectively restored the idea of a charismatic founder emperor and behaved, and he was treated very much, like an emperor with almost no limits on his power" (Gungwu 2009: 5). Both Confucianism and communism are ideologies comfortable with a social system that prizes collectivism over individualism. However, it is understanding the coexistence of capitalism with the other two Cs – Confucianism and communism – that is at the same time puzzling but so crucial to any policy towards China. A critical observer like Jonathan Fenby argued that "in today's China, the 'ism' that rules is materialism" – that is, capitalism. To him, this was represented "by the young woman on a television dating show who said that she would 'rather cry in the back of a BMW than laugh on the back of a bicycle'" (Fenby 2017: 9). The world has become familiar with images of PRC people being comfortable with a hyper-technological capitalist society where people work incredibly long hours, producing "made in" China t-shirts, shoes, and household goods dispatched to US and European markets; but also living in a dynamic megalopolis and using bullet trains among many other things. To an extent, Fenby is right, and one can see why capitalism is, among the three Cs, the most characteristic of the PRC, better known to the world than the other two. Furthermore, as Kissinger noted, the Chinese elite will never allow ideology to become an obstacle to their capitalist development and long-term goals, for instance, becoming a "modern socialist country" by 2050. This is the whole point of sinicized Marxism, a pragmatic interpretation of communist ideology. They would rather redefine the meaning of socialism with "Chinese characteristics", which should mean "whatever brought greater prosperity to China" (Kissinger 2011: 401).

Yet, if one quickly concluded that the communist elite in China have now sold their soul to capitalism – like the West did, especially after the end of the Cold War – this would lead to an incomplete and unhelpful analysis. Over recent decades we have seen the implication of this in some unrealistic expectations about China's political modernization. Indeed, as it will become clear in the next chapter, China's shift to capitalism was not just a whim so that Chinese people could wear shiny trainers, carry expensive and sophisticated phones and spend their holidays looking at art in Italy. This was also a necessity dictated by historical circumstances for which different countries in the West, together with the USSR, have been responsible. Since the First Opium War in 1839, it was clear to the Chinese imperial elite that technological development was crucial for the survival of the country. This explains a very important point in the contemporary tense dynamics between the US and China: if anything, capitalism in China was meant to strengthen rather than weaken a CCP-led society, but the West failed to understand this for too long. The Four Modernizations (四个现代化) that were central to Deng Xiaoping's agenda were goals that set out to strengthen agriculture, industry, defence, and science and technology. Liberalization of the political system and granting as many civil and human rights as there exist in western democracies was never on the agenda of post-Mao reformers.

Signs that China did not intend to liberalize, and that a communist structure of power was considered an asset rather than something to get rid of by Deng and his successors, have been around for years. To appreciate how central to the contemporary Chinese elite this type of communist state still is, one must go back to the final political verdict of the CCP on Chairman Mao. When the leader fell ill and the difficult process of handover finally resulted in the appointment of Deng Xiaoping, the latter was "ready to dump" the Chairman's economic and social policies, but not Mao's political and institutional legacy. "The Resolution on Certain Questions in the History of Our Party since the Founding of the People's Republic of China" (27 June 1981) was a sort of ruling that set the relationship between the old and new order in China. The Cultural Revolution, in the eyes of the new elite in power, was a humiliation which had impoverished the country and did not lead China to catch up with the West and free it from external aggression. The Resolution stated that "gross mistakes" were made and the "[c]hief responsibility for the grave 'Left' error of the 'cultural revolution', ... does indeed lie with Comrade Mao Zedong" (Davin 2013: 111–23). The Maoist experience had led to lack of "entrepreneurial culture", "devastation of the state's bureaucratic apparatus", and no "legal framework of property rights" (Rolf 2021: 94). This made it impossible for the PRC to develop. However, from a political and institutional viewpoint, Deng and others in the CCP salvaged the political and institutional legacy of Mao: "if we judge his activities as a whole, his contributions to the Chinese revolution far outweighs mistakes. His merits are primary and his errors secondary. He rendered indelible meritorious service in founding and building up our Party and the Chinese People's Liberation Army, in winning victory for the cause of liberation of the Chinese people, in founding the People's Republic of China and in advancing our socialist cause" (Deng & Hu: 1980–81).

A strong Communist Party was what China needed for developing quickly and for gaining respect internationally. Indeed, this made it possible for China to grow while "insulat[ing] the central state against the 'internationalisation' of its institutions" (Rolf 2021: 88). In so doing, China went through an "ongoing search" with repeated setbacks, for a workable modernization strategy while "a strong, centralized state ensured both national sovereignty and political unity" (Heilmann 2017: 24, 27). This search had started as early as China's military defeats halfway through the nineteenth century, during which a debate within the imperial elite about modernizing China began and continued amidst the competitive dialectic between communists and nationalists in the early twentieth century. They wanted the same for China, to modernize and become strong, but they wanted to pursue this objective using different prescriptions. However, it was not just China that wanted to develop: western imperialism and the relationship with the US played a crucial role in this regard.

2

"Best friends, worst enemies": China's rise and the blowback of American grand strategy

"If China remained closed, then the doors would have to be battered down."

Alan Peyrefitte

World history cannot be regarded as the sum of disconnected events. More often, it is the product of encounters between different, competing civilizations, political systems, and technologies and the tensions that exist between them. Although the Chinese elite were committed to making China great and deserve credit for the success that the PRC achieved in the post-1978 era, the West played a fundamental role in bringing it into a world capitalist economy. China's success can also be interpreted through the lens of "blowback" of European and Japanese imperialism, but most importantly US globalism. Technically, "blowback" is used by the Central Intelligence Agency (CIA) to describe the unwanted consequences of covert operations. Subsequently, it was applied by political scientist Chalmers Johnson to reflect the unintended effects – backlashes – of US foreign policy. To Johnson, "acts committed in service to an empire but never acknowledged as such have a tendency to haunt the future" and the US "cannot control the long-term effects of its policies. That is the essence of blowback" (Johnson 2002: 8, 13). This concept is essential to appreciate the responsibility that the United States' strategy-makers had for encouraging the rise of China while overlooking its long-term strategic implications.

Blowback, however, is also a constant feature of empire. Imperialism's coercion, disruption, and lack of respect for other countries or regions tend to have unpredictable and perilous consequences decades or even centuries later. China has become a great economic and military power because European and Japanese powers, even before US hegemony, had a hand in her formidable ascent. Indeed, the continuum from the eighteenth century up to China's entry into the WTO in 2001, has been that of western powers seeking to open up the Chinese economy to the world in order to profit from it. As different parts of this book show, this has come at a geopolitical cost. For good or ill, the foreign policies of imperial Britain, Japan, France, Portugal and Germany, but also the United States, have had far-reaching effects on China's process of political renovation.

THE BLOWBACK OF IMPERIALISM

Sinologists and historians continue to debate the Century of Humiliation (1839–1949), a time during which China experienced domestic turmoil and foreign aggression. The Century of Humiliation refers to the period of 110 years during which China suffered defeat in the First Opium War (1839–42) by Britain; unequal treaties; defeats and attacks by Japan, Russia, and the Eight-Nation Alliance; and the continued loss of Chinese territory with the Treaty of Versailles, among other important events. A question that remains central to the debate on the Century of Humiliation is whether this was an imperialist "carve up" of the country, or whether foreign interference was limited to coastal regions of China and did not affect the interior of the country where most people lived during this period (Elliott 2002: 143).

The answer, as usual, is probably somewhere in between. Although China was never colonized in the same way that some countries in Latin America or Africa were, imperialism undermined its power in Asia and for a time hampered its ability to prosper and innovate. Regardless, in the narrative of the Chinese elite those events still matter and continue to inform an agenda of "national rejuvenation" as a vengeance for the "intense humiliation" experienced by China, which was reduced, according to Xi Jinping, "to a semi-colonial" society after the First Opium War (Xi 2021). Simply put, the Chinese "think in terms of 'up to the Opium war' and 'after the Opium war'", seeing that event as the beginning of a tragic period in their history (Harris 1959: 162). Irrespective of whether

China was technically colonized or not, it is a fact that those years did lay bare China's sudden delay on the road to modernization compared to other regions of the world; it compelled Chinese leaders to reflect introspectively on how to overcome certain weaknesses. The Opium Wars were waged to force China to buy opium from Indian Bengal territories and to open trade routes after the Chinese Emperor had made opium illegal for over a century. Until then, the balance of trade between China and Europe was in China's favour thanks to the "export of silk, cotton, and porcelain" (Goldstone 2008: 32–3). To fund the silver and gold required to pay for those goods, Britain was "desperate" to find something that it could sell to China, as the latter "placed little value on what they saw as inferior European manufactured goods" (*ibid.*). Opium, for smoking and perdition, was the answer.

China lost the war and Hong Kong to Britain, which was only a portion of a greater price it had to pay. This loss had far-reaching consequences. However, what mattered even more was how such a loss occurred in China's first ever confrontation with a European power. This has shaped China's grand strategy up to now because it was a strategic shock. The explorer and ship captain Zheng He, a few decades before Christopher Columbus's birth, led a fleet that surpassed in size and technology the fleet used by the Italian explorer to travel to the Americas. Yet, thanks to Britain's industrial revolution, it was able to fight the Opium War with cutting-edge "iron-hulled steamships", a technology that determined the outcome of the conflict (*ibid.*: 165). *Nemesis*, the first British ship sent for war operations, had "a draft of only 5 feet" and "could operate in shallow coastal waters in virtually any wind or tidal conditions" (*ibid.*). Chinese vessels could not compete with the "maneuverability and versatility" of ships like this. The conflict marked a watershed in maritime warfare history. Until that point, China saw itself as a "celestial dynasty and imperial state" at the centre of the world (Tao 2022: vi). After the Opium Wars this was no longer the case, and that defeat has represented a wake-up call for the Chinese elite ever since.

A similar dynamic developed in China's interactions with imperial Japan, which faced its own imperialist pressures from Europe to adapt their society to ongoing changes to the world economy. While the Japanese resisted these demands until 1853, they were forced by the commodore of the American naval fleet William Perry to open up to international trade, once again thanks to the fact that the US navy "steamed" into Tokyo, known as Edo at the time: "The Japanese, quite literally, had never seen anything like it. It was their amazement at this new technology as much as the presentation of force itself that persuaded the Japanese to open their ports and sign a treaty" (Goldstone 2008: 165). The Meiji Restoration was Japan's opportunistic metamorphosis to defend the country from imperialist coercion by embracing change voluntarily. This was not so different from some of the calculations that led the Chinese elite to shift to capitalism one hundred years later. Yet, in the twentieth century Japan "quickly found its feet in the new world that was thrust upon it by the West, but China disintegrated" (White 2013: 14). The restoration in 1868 was based on a Charter Oath which sought to modernize Japanese society. The most important principles were the overcoming of ancient "customs" and the search and import of "knowledge" from the rest of the world "so as to strengthen the foundation of imperial rule" (Morton & Olenik 2005: 148). Both the geographical proximity of Japan to China and the overwhelming defeat in the First Sino-Japanese War (1894–95) – when Taiwan was first separated from the mainland – confronted China with another example of its slow progress towards modernity.

Ultimately, western and Japanese imperialism "destroyed the traditional self-image of imperial China as a culturally superior civilization at the centre of the world order", making the issue of keeping up with a modern world ever more pressing (Heilmann 2017: 23). Yet, the Chinese had a (bitter) taste of "Western political influence" and started to become familiar with ideas such as "nationalism", "Social Darwinism", "parliamentary government", the existence of an "international system of nation states", and the importance of catching up on "military technology"; awareness of all this shaped domestic debates among those who realized that China needed to catch up with the West (Mitter 2016: 17–23). At that point, the destiny of China was set: it needed to become a modern, industrialized sovereign state. The question of modernization appeared important to the declining imperial dynasty as much as to future leaders. Prince Gong, an influential Qing statesman, suggested in 1866 that Chinese students needed "to master the mysteries" of scientific subjects from mathematics to engineering, because "this, and this only, will assure the steady growth of the power of the empire"

(Kissinger 2011: 75). A few decades later, this was an objective about which both Nationalists led by Chiang Kai-shek and Communists led by Mao Zedong agreed – although, they had very different methods to achieve it. But just when Maoism succeeded in providing China with the adequate, strong, political power structure, it failed to develop China technologically and the new global hegemon, the United States, was keen to drag the PRC into the world of capitalist globalization. Today, any effort to understand the origins of current problems between China and the West should start from this highly consequential moment.

THE BLOWBACK OF AMERICAN GRAND STRATEGY

Hugh White wrote that "[i]t is as certain as such things can be that without the opening to America in 1972, China would not be where it is today" (White 2013: 20). If considered in the context of contemporary US–China geopolitical rivalry, this phrase carries a hard truth. Although China had decided to embark on a path to development in the late 1970s, the United States helped it to achieve that objective.

With the imperial powers having exhausted their resources in the destructive conflicts of the Second World War, the United States inherited the sceptre of world hegemon from Britain, whose empire was disintegrating. Differently from the UK and any other imperial power, the United States sought to expand its influence in a more subtle manner through its "Open Door" policy, and this had important implications for the future of China: "America opposed China being carved up by the Europeans and Japanese into colonial spheres of exclusive political and economic influence. Instead, it wanted China to be preserved intact, open to all comers for economic opportunities, and encouraged towards reform and modernisation along American lines" (*ibid.*: 15).

What did lay behind this strategy, and why does it continue to be relevant in contemporary US–China relations? To answer this question, it is essential to familiarize ourselves with the worldview of US President Woodrow Wilson – advocate for a League of Nations formed by independent and sovereign states after the First World War – which was deeply consequential in American grand strategy. Wilsonianism "incarnated a special (smart?) approach to nationalism" based on the triad of "peace, liberal democracy, and free markets" (Leoni 2021: 73; Tooze 2014: 44). The geopolitical implication of this worldview was to dismantle formal empires, promote democratic nation-states, while ensuring that those states abided by the new, emerging US-sponsored international regimes based on the free-market rule of law. The reason was not obscure: the United States was by far the most advanced, robust and competitive economy – certainly after the Second World War – and has remained so for several decades. In other words, if pre-Second World War empires committed their military energies to building territorial spheres of influence and ruling directly over other countries, the United States sought to organize a "global sphere of influence" (Leoni 2021: 73). This grand strategy did not require permanent occupations of other countries – although off-shore military bases represent an exception – but only military interventions and diplomatic-economic coercion to discipline recalcitrant or hostile governments, to keep anti-free-market communist forces at bay during the Cold War and to eradicate Islamist groups in the post-Cold War era. Through these lenses, Wilsonianism was, de facto, synonymous with American-designed globalism. Indeed, the "universal dominion of right" does not come for free but is attached to a "set of specifications" that goes beyond democracy itself and requires "the adoption of liberal capitalist economics", as expressed by the term "the Washington Consensus" (Quinn & Cox 2007: 500). This synergy between nationalism and globalism in US grand strategy was eloquently described by presidential candidate George W. Bush, when advocating for a "[a] distinctly American internationalism. ... Realism, in the service of American ideals" (Bush 1999).

A cynic might argue that the United States has always wanted to have it both ways. But in the Janus-faced world order described in the introduction of this book, it is not possible to have an open order without in the long-term encountering security challenges stemming from openness itself. The rise of China has confirmed this hard truth. American grand strategy and an open, LIO have benefited the United States for several decades; but it is also designed in a way that can cause structural blowbacks – not least through the rise of geopolitical rivals. In other words, American grand strategy since the end of the Second World War has tended to sow the seeds of its own decline. The United States has encouraged and supported many countries to open their economies to

the world and to embark on technological development and political lib-
eralizations, including former rivals such as Germany and Japan as well
as potential competitors like China. The integration of these three countries into the LIO was essential because they had the potential to perform
as locomotives of a global economy in which ultimately US private actors
could make billions. Not every state, however, is the same. Germany and
Japan had to renounce their geostrategic aspirations after being defeated
in the Second World War and abdicated their military policies to the
United States. It was relatively easy for Washington to use diplomatic and
financial instruments to contain the economic and technological resur-
gences of both countries. This was not possible with China.

China was not a westernized country, and it was always independent
from formal networks of US-led alliances. Furthermore, if in Germany
and Japan the state played an influential role in organizing national
developmental objectives, in China the state played an even bigger role.
Yet, the US was too focused on achieving the objectives of its Open Door
policy and – in the last two decades of the Cold War – on preventing the
USSR from finding new allies.

The US believed – particularly, since the end of the Cold War and
until the early Obama administration – that it could get China to accept
the rules of the Washington Consensus; that it was going to privatize its
economy and open it to the global economy; and that this would have to
go hand-in-hand with political liberalization and democratization. The
PRC's growth brought to the fore the tension between geopolitical and
geoeconomic interests that constitutes the LIO, as the US increasingly
struggled to keep the world open enough for American and global business while "prevent[ing] the rise of any grand challenge" to American
power (Harvey 2003: 84). Was this a genuine strategic mistake or were
economic interests too lucrative for strategic calculations to restrain
them – especially after the Soviet threat had disappeared?

US–CHINA RELATIONS DURING THE COLD WAR: FROM RAPPROCHEMENT TO NORMALIZATION

Following the Century of Humiliation, the tragic results of the Great
Leap Forward and the Cultural Revolution promoted by Mao Zedong in

the 1960s made that need for catching up with modern Western powers even more urgent for the PRC. This was the objective of Deng Xiaoping in the aftermath of Mao's death. Even before that, however, Mao was concerned with the geostrategic environment China faced. From the pending threat of a Soviet invasion to territorial disputes with India, from the US war in Vietnam to unfavourable events in Taiwan and Tibet, not to mention rivalry with the US, Mao's agenda was curtailed. But if China had managed to maintain the balance of power and to dodge the bullet of a Soviet invasion, it was noted that this was only because of Cold War dynamics and rivalries between China's enemies themselves (Kissinger 2011: 200–1). Therefore, China was eager to find common ground with the United States.

After Mao Zedong's decision to side with the "soviet-led anti-imperialist camp" in the late 1940s, many in the United States believed that this was the "loss of China" (Tao 2022: 376). Yet, two decades later a thaw in the relationship was in both Chinese and American elites' own interests. Following an invitation by the PRC's Premier Zhou Enlai, the US elite made a courageous move. The history of Henry Kissinger's secret trip in July 1971 that initiated a new relationship between the US and China is well known. More interesting is what drove the American elite to make such an audacious move and to confirm Nixon's China policy in the following decades. To understand this, one must travel back to the four years that preceded Kissinger's trip.

In October 1967, presidential candidate Nixon shared his foreign policy views in the journal *Foreign Affairs*. In a highly consequential article, Nixon contextualized his intervention by explaining that Asia "around the rim of China" was undergoing a transformation; that "communism is not necessarily the wave of Asia's future"; and that the region offered opportunities for capitalism as it was "becoming Western without ceasing to be Asian" (Nixon 1967: 111–2). Although the speech was clearly pitched with a strong anti-communist tone and China was portrayed as the "threat" to the region, Nixon laid out a few key points: "Taking the long view, we simply *cannot afford* to leave China forever outside the family of nations, there to nurture its fantasies, cherish its hates and threaten its neighbours. There is no place on this small planet for a billion of its potentially most able people to live in angry isolation" (*ibid*.: 121, emphasis added).

Four years later, these words paved the way to the rapprochement, which in its first round ended with the Joint Communiqué of the United States of America and the People's Republic of China (28 February 1972), also known as the "Shanghai Communiqué". In the latter it was established that "economic relations based on equality and mutual benefit are in the interest of the peoples of the two countries", that "there is but one China and that Taiwan is a part of China" (*ibid.*). Although this was nothing like an "open door", it represented a major step forward. China was certainly instrumental for the US, as Washington wanted to impede the USSR from acquiring a powerful ally. This, however, was just part of the story, and compared to creating a global world order, victory against the USSR was the tactical objective, a means to an end. In a memorandum to Nixon dated 25 March 1971, Kissinger confirmed that, as requested, he was working towards the removal of "obstacles to personal and commercial contacts", with the aim of relaxing controls over "currency", "oil companies", "cargoes", and "aircraft sales" among other parts of trade (Kissinger 1971). Indeed, Kissinger noted in his "diary" that Nixon saw the rapprochement to China as "part of an overall strategic design, not a shopping list of mutual irritations"; and that while there was also a tactical logic to undermine the USSR, the US–China relationship "evolved to where it became central to the evolution of the new global order" (Kissinger 2011: 235, 243). Much later, in a memorandum to President Ronald Reagan in 1982, the former president Nixon sought to temper the charisma of the Hollywood star noting that while the eventuality of a Soviet aggression continued to be key to US–China relations, "the major unifying factor which will draw us closer together in the next decade could well be our economic interdependence" (*ibid.*: 393).

All in all, it was suggested that "[p]robably only a president with Nixon's impeccably anti-communist credentials could have got away with [the rapprochement]" (White 2013: 22). Nonetheless, the opening of the PRC was as necessary for the PRC – whose "Four Modernizations of agriculture, industry, science and technology, and the military" began in December 1978 – as it was for any American government (Wang 2021: 221). Furthermore, it was more than a personal achievement as demonstrated by the fact that the following decades showed a great deal of continuity, especially from the US and the White House in particular – which was counterbalanced by Congress.

The rapprochement achieved in 1972 represented just the anteroom of, ideally, a more comprehensive process of normalization. Even after the Mao–Nixon meeting, there continued to be an uncomfortable anomaly caused by US formal recognition of Taiwan as "the legitimate government of China" (Kissinger 2011: 350). Therefore, on 17 May 1978 Carter was determined to assign "high priority" to China in its foreign policy agenda. On the one hand, he sent another big shot in American diplomacy – NSA Zbigniew Brzezinski – to Beijing to communicate that Carter wanted to continue Nixon's agenda. On the other hand, President Carter and Deng Xiaoping succeeded in developing the rapprochement into a "normalization" of relations by resolving the issue of Taiwan. Beijing was finally recognized as the capital of the PRC, a decision officialized with the relocation of the American embassy to mainland China from Formosa Island (Taiwan) – while "a diplomat from Beijing would replace Taipei's representative in Washington" (*ibid.*: 356). This change was the substance of the second communiqué, known as the Joint Communiqué on the Establishment of Diplomatic Relations (1 January 1979). Nonetheless, the issue of US arms sales to Taiwan remained unresolved. This was partly due to unclear communication of intents between Chinese and American negotiators, but also because of the hurry both countries were in to achieve such normalization, Deng Xiaoping's commitment to allow China to access international services, technology and know-how, and US domestic politics concerns (Foot 2005: 104–9).

Continuity in US foreign policy towards China, however, was not smooth. Carter's action set a pattern of US China policy-making for the following decades, characterized by frictions between the White House and Congress. The former seemed to be more focused on achieving grand strategic goals whereas the latter was more concerned with counterbalancing the White House and upholding democratic principles. Indeed, the Taiwan Relations Act of 1979 was voted on by Congress to assert its supervision of "normalization" and to counterbalance the diplomatic downgrading of Taiwan. The Act reaffirmed the importance of sustaining democracy and human rights on the island, and above all to support Taipei by providing "defense articles and defense services in such quantity as may be necessary" (H.R.2479 – Taiwan Relations Act).

Carter's policy was, however, facilitated by Deng Xiaoping's economic reforms, a move that created interest in the US business community. As Kissinger recalls, during the Chairman's visit to the US in January and February 1979 he met with "heads of Coca-Cola, PepsiCo, and General Motors ... shook hands with members of the Harlem Globetrotters basketball team ... played to the crowd at a rodeo and barbecue in Simonton, Texas, donning a ten-gallon hat and riding in a stagecoach ... toured manufacturing and technology facilities, including a Ford assembly plant in Hapeville, Georgia; the Hughes Tool Company in Houston ... and the Boeing plant outside Seattle" (Kissinger 2011: 361). The supreme leader wanted the bottom line of his trip to be that China was seeking to acquire foreign – western – technology, to "get to know all about American life" and to "absorb everything" that benefited the PRC (*ibid.*: 371–3). Deng's trip to the US made an impact on investors. Coupled with mutual Sino-American fear of the USSR, this led to "unprecedently close cooperation" – which also included American indirect support to the Khmer Rouge and to a spirit of cooperation that now seems more distant than it actually is (*ibid.*).

As the PRC led by Deng moved coherently towards economic development, Ronald Reagan – Carter's successor – brought the ambiguity of American foreign policy towards China to a new high. On the one hand, Reagan "avoided criticizing the rapprochement with China" while attacking the USSR; however, this low-profile stance towards the PRC was balanced by an assertive rhetoric about defending democracy in Taiwan, a less direct attack on China (*ibid.*: 379). As Kissinger put it, he "embodied the existing American ambivalence" where an unquestionable, "powerful commitment to the new relationship with Beijing coexisted with a strong residue of emotional support for Taiwan" (*ibid.*: 380). This point made by the former NSA to President Nixon is of paramount importance because this ambivalence has continued to characterize US's China policy into the early 2020s. Reagan's approach to China, therefore, betrayed that highly challenging conundrum of choosing between economic and security interests. Indeed, after Reagan, using an ambiguous phrase, advocated for "official relations" with Taiwan, he then had to send George H. Bush, his vice-presidential candidate and former liaison officer to China, for a clarifying meeting with Deng, who was furious. Bush told Deng that Reagan was not trying to undermine the "normalization" process. This, however, was not enough to reassure the supreme leader that the new American administration intended to abide by the agenda brought forward by Nixon. Therefore, Reagan asked Kissinger – probably, the PRC's closest friend among US strategists – to meet the Chinese ambassador in Washington, DC, Chai Zemin, for what Kissinger described as a "tall order" (*ibid.*: 380–1).

Nonetheless, the Reagan administration oversaw the signing of a third communiqué, known as the August 17 communiqué (1982) in which everything agreed in the previous two was confirmed. This communiqué, however, failed to settle the military relationship between the US and Taiwan. The Chinese elite did not intend to put in writing that they would resolve the Taiwan issue peacefully if the US stopped its arms sale to Taiwan; meanwhile, the US did not want to set a hard deadline for ending military support (Harding 1992: 115). Ultimately, they agreed to the US selling weapons to Taiwan, so long as they did not "exceed, either in qualitative or in quantitative terms, the level of those supplied in recent years since the establishment of diplomatic relations between the United States and China"; and that the sale of weapons would gradually end. To Kissinger, Reagan's China and Taiwan policy was one of incomprehensible contradictions (Kissinger 2011: 385). In reality, this was just the beginning of a dilemma that was difficult to resolve, especially if the US did not want to give up the economic opportunities offered by the potentially huge Chinese market.

FROM BUSH SENIOR TO BUSH JUNIOR: THE STRATEGIC OVERSIGHT OF CHINA

The absence of an existential threat to the US at the end of the Cold War made the friction between the two sides – economic and security interests – of the US' China policy more problematic. In the two decades between 1989 and the Obama administration's pivot to Asia in 2011, the US often let economic interests prevail over strategic calculations and values. Following the violent repression of the Tiananmen Square protests by the CCP, President George H. Bush's reaction was not the one of a commander-in-chief of a world committed to promote democracy worldwide. Bush, similar to Reagan, wanted to "condemn" those actions "while also remaining engaged with China" (Bush & Scowcroft 1998: 89–90). At first, he suspended some diplomatic and military exchanges – including sales – although there were not many between the two countries at that point. Bush also announced opposition to China within the World Bank. However, he felt it necessary to write a personal letter "addressing Deng 'as a friend' and bypassing the bureaucracy and his own ban on high-level exchanges" (Kissinger 2011: 416). With a deeply apologetic tone, Bush was genuflecting to China's Chairman. The letter shows this in several passages. The US president told Deng that he was writing to him "in a spirit of genuine friendship … a genuine 'lao pengyou'"; and that Bush was buck-passing responsibilities of criticisms against the CCP's handling of Tiananmen Square's demonstrations onto the US and the international community rather than the White House (Standoff at Tiananmen 2012). Indeed, Bush stated that certain events "captured the imagination of the entire world" (*ibid.*). Yet, he highlighted that this must not "undermine a vital relationship patiently built up over the past seventeen years" (*ibid.*). Hugh White argued that this apologetic stance "seem[ed] to have been more a last application of old Cold War strategic logic than a first indication of new calculations" (2013: 23). However, White's statement implies that Bush had concerns of a sudden shift in Chinese foreign policy closer to the USSR. This was unwarranted, and the main concern was economic. The *Wall Street Journal* recalled those moments and pointed out how for Bush it was soon "time to look beyond the [Tiananmen] moment to important and enduring aspects of this vital relationship for the United States" (Baker 2019). Ironically, when George W. Bush's father died in 2018, Xi Jinping stated that he was "greatly saddened" and that George H. Bush was "someone who made important contributions to the China–US friendship and relationship" (Westcott & George 2018).

The end of the Cold War had important implications for Sino-American relations. The main change was the defeat of the Soviet Union. Chinese people could sleep soundly at night as a land invasion through its inner flanks was off the list of threats. However, this shift carried major consequences in US foreign policy. In 2013, White argued that the US' China policy of hedging "has failed" because "[n]ow it is too late" to contain the rise of China (White 2013: 26–7). He asked "[h]ow did this happen?", 9/11 aside, he blamed a worldview which believed the

United States "had become unchallengeable"; he noted that "so many" were "so blind" as most people did not "comprehend the scale, speed and significance of China's rise" (*ibid.*). The answer to White's question should be sought in the post-Cold War years. The West's victory against Soviet communism misled many to believe that it was the "end of history". This paradigm for the new world order had several facets. From a military perspective, it was argued that it was time for a "strategic pause" (Freedman 1998: 5). Indeed, nation-states were perceived as withering away as actors and forces of globalization, whereas geostrategic logics of the Cold War were quickly becoming obsolete since there was no other state capable of threatening democracies, let alone the US.

The United States saw this as a once-in-a-lifetime opportunity to expand the LIO – that is, to pursue geoeconomic openness – as a way of extending its hegemony, especially during the years of the Clinton administration. Anthony Lake, Bill Clinton's NSA announced that "[t] he successor to a doctrine of containment must be a strategy of enlargement" (Lake 1993: 5). Regarding the PRC, this strategy translated into the Clinton administration's effort to drag Beijing into the WTO, hoping to tap the Chinese market (Leoni 2021: 78).

Initially, Clinton adopted a pragmatic approach by wanting China in the global economy as long as political and economic liberalization was on track. This was pursued as Clinton sought to tie "China's Most Favored Nation" trade status to progress in China's human rights record (Kissinger 2011: 465). This ultimately led to China's entry into the WTO in December 2001. In his speech to convince Congress, Clinton stated that "most of the critics of the China W.T.O. agreement do not seriously question its economic benefits" (Clinton 2000). The conclusive line was unequivocable: "if you believe in a future of greater openness and freedom for the people of China ... If you believe in a future of greater prosperity for the American people, you certainly should be for this agreement. ... It's an historic opportunity and a profound American responsibility. I'll do all I can to convince Congress and the American people to support it" (*ibid.*).

As *The Economist* noted, on the tenth anniversary of the PRC's membership, Clinton's promises were a disappointment for liberals (*The Economist* 2011b). Yet, both foreigners and Americans "prospered" in the subsequent decade as "American foreign direct investment reaps returns of 13.5% in China, compared with 9.7% worldwide" (*The Economist* 2011a). Clinton, in his speech to Congress, had also maintained that "[b]y lowering the barriers that protect state-owned industries, China is speeding a process that is removing government from vast areas of people's lives. ... That system was a big source of the Communist Party's power" (Clinton 2000). This however, confirmed a major misunderstanding in the West about China. However, as it was confirmed by Jiang Zemin, post-Deng China continued to open up to the world economy while expecting "respect for the political system and development path chosen by individual nation-states", meaning that political reforms were not going to follow from economic reforms, contrary to what liberal doctrines theorize (Wang 2021: 249–50).

Ultimately, with the Cold War over, it could be said that geopolitical interests were "significantly marginalized in favor of the economic calculus" by the acceleration of US-led globalization (Smith 2006: 187). This policy, however, contained the seeds of "blowback". Clinton's docile foreign policy allowed China to silently grow. In the following years this opened a debate in the West about whether the right strategy was "engagement" or "containment" – a discussion that continues today (Breslin 2004: 416). The latest version of Bill Clinton's national security strategy warned that China was rising and that this presented several challenges, but for the former governor of Arkansas it was too late to act on it (NSS 2000: 64). As a result, George W. Bush and his incoming foreign policy team were eager to deal with the rise of China. Noting that unipolarity was quickly being eroded, Bush demanded that a greater dose of "realism" should have been injected into US foreign policy (Bush 1999). China was initially portrayed as "a competitor, not a strategic partner" that needed to be "unthreatened, but not unchecked" (Bush 1999). To Condoleezza Rice, Bush's would-be secretary of state, it was a "potential threat" because China wanted to "alter Asia's balance of power in its own favour" (Rice 2000: 56). However, after a US spy plane collided with a Chinese jet, Bush stated that "[w]e should not let this incident destabilize relations" (Bush 2001). When asked about the "balance that you think should be struck between our strategic interests and our economic interests in Asia", Bush replied that China needed "to be a trading partner of ours" (*ibid.*). It was argued that since the beginning, the Bush administration intended to operate a strategic shift towards

Asia – anticipating Obama's pivot to Asia by ten years (Silove 2016: 54–5). Yet, 9/11 continued to reproduce that post-Cold War view of the world in which the contemporary international security environment was characterized by a clash of civilizations; and by conflicts where the West fought non-state actors and enemies in areas of instability such as failed states. A Pentagon map represented the geopolitical world order as divided between developed and unstable countries – in the latter, terrorism prospered amid failed and rogue states (Barnett 2004). The major policy direction on China came as late as 2006, when the deputy secretary of state Robert Zoellick delivered his "responsible stakeholder" speech (2005), delivered in the early days of the second Bush administration, after 9/11. The speech signalled a shift in focus to great power relations and it could be seen as a final call for China to modernize not only economically but also politically.

THE OBAMA–TRUMP CHINA POLICY

China was not a priority even in the very early stages of the Obama administration. Indeed, the handover from Bush to Obama in the 2007/08 biennium and the following years were still dominated, as Obama's first national security strategy demonstrates, by the Great Recession (2008), the increase of American troops in Afghanistan, the unravelling of the Iraq war, and terrorism. But while the United States was bogged down in these problems, China's power was growing, to the point that 2009–10 was recorded as the "year of assertiveness" as Beijing adopted a more confrontational stance over different territorial disputes and over North Korea (Shambaugh 2020: 16).

This, however, was the legacy of the policies from the previous decade, and the Obama administration was able to progressively change the priorities of the United States. Indeed, Obama decided to take the bull by the horns and launched his signature policy, the "pivot to Asia". Although this was overall a mild effort, the policy marked an unequivocal shift in US foreign policy towards China, and it clearly aimed at preventing Beijing from achieving regional hegemony in Asia. The "pivot" had three prongs: diplomatic, economic and military – signalling that the rise of China was structural and its implications far-reaching. Diplomatically,

Obama sought to strengthen US ties with India, Japan, Australia, and the Association of Southeast Asian Nations (ASEAN)'s members to encircle China. Economically, his administration promoted the Trans-Pacific Partnership (TPP). Among other things, this mega-regional, multilateral framework was aimed at creating an area of trade based on free-market, labour, and environmental standards that excluded China. The objective was that of disciplining the CCP and compelling it to reform its economy; and above all to privatize the strategic sectors of the Chinese economy while breaking the link between party and industries. Finally, from a military viewpoint, the rise of a powerful China in the western Pacific demanded more attention from Washington, and this led to a shift from a 50/50 distribution of US naval assets between the Atlantic and the Indo-Pacific to a 40/60 ratio.

From many points of view, especially if looking at their style and ideologies, Obama and Trump were two incompatible leaders. Yet, Trump, like Obama, also put China at the very centre of his foreign policy. But by the time Trump reached the White House it was clear that Obama's "pivot" had not had any impact on China's rise, and specifically that China had no intentions to either liberalize its economy further or backtrack from its claims in the South China Sea (Leoni 2021: 222–3). Therefore, Trump's agenda was characterized by a more aggressive version of Obama's China policy. Diplomatically, Trump continued the "pivot to Asia" but changed the name to Free and Open Indo-Pacific (FOIP). It had two objectives: on the one hand, "free and open" recovered an old theme in US political tradition, the opposition to authoritarianism and empire; on the other, Indo-Pacific was meant to charm India, which was rightly considered as a game-changer in the great geopolitical game of the region. Economically, Trump also pressed China to reform its domestic political-economic model, but he did so in a confrontational and bilateral fashion: he increased trade tariffs on millions of Chinese products imported into the US. Militarily, he endorsed the geostrategic rebalancing of Obama but advocated an increase in the number of US ships; this better served US interests in a region where the biggest navy in the world – the Chinese one – operates, although it is unclear whether this increase will happen (*ibid.*: ch. 6).

The Trump era has been considered by many as a departure from the American grand strategy exercised in previous years. Yet, as far as it concerns China, not only was his foreign policy in great continuity with Obama, it also unveiled an uncomfortable reality, that the United States does not intend to be a proactive element of the LIO if the latter does not benefit its national economy. China's nationalist approach to the global economy – and its military assertiveness in the South China Sea – has eroded the competitive and structural advantage gained by the United States since the end of Second World War.

As the final chapter of this book will show, the Obama–Trump China policy has continued into the Biden administration which, with the Build Back Better World (B3W) strategy, has conflated the multilateralism of Obama with the nationalism of Trump, seeking to create a new US-led sphere of influence in the West. Before we do that, it is worth looking more closely at the extent to which China has managed to succeed globally vis-à-vis the West, since the picture remains uneven and evolving.

3

Successes and limits of China's engagement with the world economy

"There is no simple disengagement path, given the scope of economic and legal entanglements. This isn't a 'trade' we can simply walk away from".

John Mauldin

At the end of the 2010s, Martin Jacques predicted China would "rule the world" and the "end of the Western world" (2009). Elsewhere I argued that Jacques's claim about a new world order is materializing (Leoni 2021: ch. 4). Yet, it is too soon to confirm Jacques's claims, especially about China ruling the world. About a decade ago, David Shambaugh disagreed with Jacques because "China has an increasingly broad 'footprint' across the globe, but it is not particularly deep" (2013: 5–6). Apart from some important exceptions, China's economic presence in other countries is not enough to provide Beijing with structural political leverage, unlike that of the US, which has become hegemonic through the dollar. On the other hand, the PRC can damage certain industries in other countries and indirectly exert pressure on governments; furthermore, while China's economic expansion remains superficial it is growing fast as the eurozone struggles to emerge from more than a decade of financial austerity. This has led both China hawks and the media to suggest that the PRC is committed to a sort of neocolonialism through investments and acquisition of foreign assets. There certainly is an element of truth in this, as I explore below, but one has to consider both sides of the coin. This chapter argues that while China has eroded the West's productive power in some areas, its success remains limited and uneven. This argument balances some of the claims set out in Chapter 2, but also making the reader reflect on the complexity of China's rise to great power. Here and in the following chapter, it is shown that ultimately, operating in a LIO is no picnic, that is, it offers challenges and not just success. This is even more the case at a time when the West has started to see the drawbacks, in addition to the benefits, of interacting with China.

THE BELT AND ROAD INITIATIVE AND OVERSEAS INTERESTS: CHINA GOES GLOBAL?

Since 1978 the PRC has used its foreign policy to protect its path towards development from both external interferences and military invasions. This entailed, above all, normalizing relations with the US to obtain additional guarantees that the Soviet Union would not attack the country via its long border, while importing western technology to strengthen the economic, military and institutional basis of the country. Instead, since 2008, China has been able to "leverage its growing economic power to achieve foreign policy objectives" (Norris 2016: 44). It has used its cheap and vast availability of labour and huge market to "enhance the regime's legitimacy while demonstrating to China's international partners the benefits of China's growing stature" (*ibid.*: 55).

The Belt and Road Initiative (BRI), a heavily funded, gargantuan project for infrastructural interconnectivity that stretches between the PRC, Eurasia and the Indo-Pacific, has represented the signature policy for implementing China's foreign economic strategy. Indeed, China's foreign minister Wang Yi has said that this is President Xi's most important project. Defining the BRI is a challenge in itself, worthy of more in-depth academic exploration. The term and its focus are ever-evolving, as I explain below. Tracking all the low-level ramifications of this policy is a major endeavour. Nonetheless, there are important issues that can be unpacked when looking at the BRI from a big picture perspective. The Belt seeks to promote connectivity across the Eurasian landmass through railways, highways and economic corridors; the Road – rather confusingly – seeks to achieve the same by investing in ports and commercial routes from the South China Sea to the north of the Indian Ocean (Miller 2017: 12; Belt and Road Forum for International Cooperation).

This policy responds to two broad grand strategic objectives, which I list here in order of importance and timespan for achievements.

Economically, the BRI facilitates China's mercantilist approach to globalization, necessary to increase the export of over-accumulated goods and capital while protecting national industries; it secures imports of energy resources and foodstuffs for a fast-growing, consumerist society; it also makes partners more dependent on trade with Beijing. Geostrategically, the BRI can help China resolve its maritime vulnerability. Building a network of transport routes and infrastructure across Eurasia will allow China to bypass – if necessary – the hostile waters of the Indian Ocean, where the People's Liberation Army Navy (PLAN) does not have the logistical infrastructure to operate and defend China's trade in deep and trafficked waters thousands of miles from home (Frankopan 2015: 516).

In the process of achieving this, the "going out" philosophy implicit in the BRI could allow China to achieve two more objectives: acquiring or integrating with western industries so that Beijing can obtain technological know-how and exporting China's image and culture by becoming more influential in other countries' economic affairs – through cultural institutions such as the Confucius Institute – or by simply improving the standing of more Chinese brands. While this is not the main objective of the BRI, such external engagement will also weaken the influence of China's biggest rival, the United States: it will charm potential western partners and drawing them into the Sinosphere. This is already happening, as I discuss in the final chapter, despite human rights violations in Xinjiang, the mismanagement of the Covid-19 crisis, and China's position on the Russian invasion of Ukraine. Increasingly Beijing sees the developing world as a more unrestrained space for building its sphere of influence, at a time when building partnerships overseas has become a grand strategic imperative for China's power projection. Beijing's siren song and the Global South's authoritarian-friendly environment enable China to achieve different objectives, such as establishing bonds necessary to secure favourable votes inside multilateral institutions, or allowing its military navy to use ports for logistical purposes. This is crucial for China to achieve strategic depth beyond South-East Asia.

Speaking of diplomatic success, although many detractors do not buy Xi Jinping's slogans about an eventual China-led order based on harmony between people, the BRI has already achieved a very important goal: it has been endorsed by the most important institution of the LIO, the United Nations (UN). The latter has acknowledged that the BRI can support progress of the international community with its "five priority areas for international cooperation". Although the BRI is different from the 2030 Agenda of the UN Development Programme, the UN stated that "they share in many respects a similar vision and some basic principles" in the fight against poverty (UNDESA). Whether one believes this or not, it is nonetheless a major victory for China.

The success of the BRI, however, needs to be unpacked further. Although the BRI is clearly an ambitious, well-resourced, large-scale project that is connecting China to the world, it is not without criticism. The West has unwittingly contributed to this success by helping China create a brand rather than a coherent set of policies. First, the US's hawkish representation of the BRI as China's strategy for "global domination" has promoted international awareness about the risks of this project but it has also "helped Beijing burnish the BRI brand" (Storey 2021).

Second, China has proved particularly skilful in "choreograph[ing] public diplomacy" to sell the BRI to its potential partners using memoranda of understanding; often, these memoranda contain little economic substance but can pave the way to future economic and political cooperation (*ibid.*). So even though there is evidence that the EU's foreign direct investments in ASEAN and Africa are higher than those of China, few people are aware of this. Clearly, China has been more adept than others at showcasing its successes. As Sven Biscop put it, the BRI is "[t]he project that the whole world talks about ... Nobody is talking about Russia's Eurasian Economic Union, the EU's EU-Asia Connectivity Strategy, or the US' Blue Dot Network" (Biscop 2021: 125).

Third, the western media has been instrumental in amplifying the narrative of the BRI. It has been particularly keen to attach the BRI label to most Chinese international activities and investments; yet, there is not necessarily always a political control room behind every investment. The BRI can be "difficult to pinpoint" because it seems to be used to describe "anything that China achieves with any country" (*ibid.*: 126). As a former British diplomat to China told me, "we must not call it the BRI". The very (banal) act of using the acronym is a victory for the CCP, and it also allows the party to showcase a strategic foresight that often does not exist. This makes even more sense if looked through the lens of "frag-mented authoritarianism" (Mertha 2009: 996). This scholarly framework has, since 1988, found large consensus within the academic community. It maintains that while in China there is an authoritarian political centre that dictates policy – especially over a few core interests and ideological principles – decision-making is watered down by the "parochial organ-izational and political goals" of agencies, leaders, regions and provinces that are at a lower level of the CCP's hierarchy (*ibid.*). The further away these are from the political centre, the more difficult it is for the CCP politburo to enforce its policy, to prevent challenges and to prevail over personal interests (*ibid.*). With the BRI's operations happening far from the political centre of China, fragmentation can play a significant role eroding the Beijing elite's ability to coordinate economic with security interests.

Following from this, one might say that there is something enigmatic about the BRI. Initially the BRI was not originally conceived of as it exists today. It might be argued that it represents the latest articulation of a process that was initially aimed at developing China's poor west-ern provinces; subsequently, this strategy incorporated Central Asia, and with the concept of the New Silk Road, it stretched to Europe and the Middle East. The reference to silk carried important historical res-onance of a prosperous China and of its role in connecting Asia and Europe together through the trade of this precious fabric (Frankopan 2015: 8–11), recalling a China-led world order. But "[a]s ambitions grew, what was first known as One Belt, One Road (OBOR) then as BRI came to encompass six major overland 'corridors'", to which one should add its maritime articulations through the Indo-Pacific Ocean and the Arctic (Biscop 2021: 126).This vignette captures China's smart and pragmatic approach of "adjusting by doing", which allows the CCP to be flexible not only in the way it operates but also in the way it communicates its successes to international audiences. The very long-term objectives of China's grand strategy and the BRI allow the CCP to escape scrutiny and accountability because some projects are still to be realized.

On the other hand, not every economic operation with a Chinese company involved is "directed from the top down" and cannot always be linked back to the BRI, to policy interests or to a geopolitical strategy (Jones & Hameiri 2020). Furthermore, not every BRI-related operation is successful. *Nikkei Asia*, the world's most circulated financial news-paper, pointed out that while Chinese investments in Africa appear to have paid dividends, it is possible that the PRC could have achieved similar results "without committing nearly $200 billion in bilateral loans and FDI in a distant continent full of political and economic risks" (Pei 2020). The paper noted that "China might not have paid more for the same raw materials" if it bought it from the market, and that hopes that direct control of resources might lead to better deals and guarantees is "illusory" (*ibid*). The *Global Times* itself – a CCP-sponsored paper that also publishes in English – admitted that a "lack of experience and capability with overseas investment, remain the key impediments for Chinese companies trying to expand abroad" (Phoenix Weekly 2015).

Another point worth considering is that the BRI has not found much opposition beyond political rhetoric, and only recently have the United States, Australia and other countries been looking at Chinese invest-ments and acquisitions with greater scrutiny. This is an important point. Indeed, no matter how rapacious Beijing's foreign economic policy might be, the PRC is not a colonial power of the likes of fifteenth-century Spain, nineteenth-century Britain, twentieth-century Japan and even the US after the Second World War. Rather, China takes advantage of the fact that the developing world needs financial support to close the gap, while the developed world has been living through more than a decade of financial austerity and it struggles not to accept "easy" cash.

This requires looking at the BRI with a sober rather than ideological view. On the one hand, Jonathan Hoslag is right to raise awareness of the risks of an imbalanced relationship between China and Europe, which he captures with the phrase "Silk Road Trap". It is true that the economic relationship with the PRC needs to be informed more by long-term and strategic thinking; the negative implications of China's mercantilist for-eign economic policy should also be considered more seriously than has been done so far, and acted upon. On the other hand, it is unfair to label the BRI a "trap". As Lee Jones and Shahar Hameiri have argued in their report for Chatham House, "[r]ecipient governments cannot expect China to carry out due diligence on their behalf" (Jones & Hameiri 2020). It is the responsibility of whoever accepts a loan or sells an asset to consider the implications of certain economic operations.

Take, for instance, the Oscar-winning documentary *American Factory*, first produced by Barack and Michelle Obama and distributed by Netflix. The documentary tells the story of a glass production plant opened by the Chinese Fuyao Glass Industry Group Co., Ltd. in Ohio. The location is important because the same plant used to be run by General Motors where workers were paid twice what they currently earn. The state of Ohio even provided Fuyao with incentives to open the plant there. The main lesson from this is that local stakeholders, due to the financial crisis, accepted worse conditions to avoid unemployment. While it feels harsh to blame this on workers, responsibility cannot only be attributed to China. Examples like this abound in the everyday life of the BRI. As Biscop put it, the Great Recession in 2008 was a major turning point because it "left China relatively unscathed, allowing it to play a key role in restarting the global economy while the US and the EU were hit hard" (2021: 30).

CHINA'S ECONOMIC STRENGTHS VIS-À-VIS THE WEST

China's economic power in the international order must be assessed by considering how exposed other countries are to both the political whims and economic disruption originating in the PRC. The length of this book does not allow for a comprehensive survey, but there are certainly some areas of major concern with particularly evident strategic implications for the West. The most structural and consequential factor of dependency is the sheer size of the Chinese market. The PRC's GDP was $15.66 trillion in 2020, only $5 trillion short of US GDP. More interestingly, China's middle class, according to a Pew survey, has "swell[ed] from 39.1 million people (3.1 percent of the population) in 2000 to roughly 707 million (50.8 percent of the population) in 2018" (China Power Team 2017). These numbers have a fatal attraction for companies in search of lucrative markets. Throughout the 2010s, China's GDP doubled, while Xi announced in late 2020 that China will double its GDP again by 2035. There is every possibility that the PRC "stands a good chance" of achieving this, as it would only require a GDP annual growth of 4.7 per cent for 15 years – it is too soon to say if Xi Jinping's commitment to a zero-Covid policy will change these projections (Lee 2021).

Amidst this positive scenario, it has been assessed that throughout the world "[a]lmost all [industrial] sectors are exposed to China" (McKinsey Global Institute 2019: 7). According to the report *China and the World*, China "accounts for more than 20 percent of global consumption in 17 out of 20 categories in manufacturing" while its "share of services consumption has also increased"; any company seeking to expand its business "may not be able to afford to overlook opportunities in China" (*ibid.*). This seems an accurate statement, as confirmed by the annual survey of the European Chamber of Commerce in China, conducted among 585 companies who operate in China. To the question "[i]s your company considering shifting current or planned investments in China to other markets?", 91 per cent confirmed that this is not an option now (ECCC 2021: 11). This number is striking because not only is it higher than in previous years, it also coincided with a time when the PRC was under pressure because of the CCP mishandling of the pandemic as well as concerns over Xinjiang and the National Security Law in Hong Kong. To the question "[h]ow would you describe the business outlook for your sector in China over the next two years?", 68 per cent responded "optimistic", 25 per cent were "neutral" and only 6 per cent were "pessimistic"; in 2013 there had been a slightly higher number of optimistic companies (*ibid.*: 9).

This perception of China within the international business community and the competitive nature of the Chinese market itself bears great responsibility for the deindustrialization of the West – discussed in more detail below – and for creating other vulnerabilities. An area that should be of particular concern to anybody looking at China's economic power through a strategic lens is that of pharmaceuticals. Here, the United States is particularly exposed. It imports about 80 per cent of its pharmaceutical ingredients and "most of these come from China" (Whiton 2020). At a testimony to the US Senate on Covid-19, Stephen W. Schondelmeyer, professor of pharmaceutical management and economics placed the "heavy dependence upon foreign sources for drug production" as the principal vulnerability in the resilience of national health (Schondelmeyer 2021: 7). China plays a major role in this area. Schondelmeyer noted that in the Hubei province alone there are "37 pharmaceutical factories that held Drug Master Files for making active pharmaceutical ingredients (APIs) for US drug products", and that these plants produce "ibuprofen, hydromorphone, metoprolol, metformin, zidovudine, azithromycin, clindamycin, and levofloxacin" (*ibid*.: 6). Furthermore, China makes "nearly all" supplies of penicillin G and about 80 per cent of the world's supply of antibiotics (*ibid*.: 7). In a different testimony, Rosemary Gibson, co-author of *China Rx: Exposing the Risks of America's Dependence on China for Medicine*, said that generic drugs represent "90 percent of the medicines that Americans take" (Gibson 2019: 1). She noted that even if the US was to buy pharmaceuticals from India, this would not be a viable solution: Indian generic manufacturers "depend on China for 80 percent of the active ingredients and chemical intermediates essential for production" (*ibid*.).

In this industrial sector, therefore, China is a player you would not want to mess with. But the story of pharmaceuticals has two additional lessons, one of which concerns supply chains more directly. The outbreak of African swine fever among Chinese pigs in 2019 raised concerns within the US Congress about disruption to the supply of heparin, an anticoagulant derived from pig intestines (Rees 2019). Similar – although less worrying – problems have been experienced with imports of goods like cars or phones. By looking at the pharmaceutical sector it is possible to gain insights into the US loss of industrial capacity to China and the rest of the world. For instance, Gibson reported that the last US penicillin fermentation plant was closed in 2004 because, like companies in other countries, this sector was put out of business by China's cheap sales (*ibid*.). But one should consider that while China is a rapacious economic player, western capitalism was no less rapacious when those plants were closed in the name of profit.

Pharmaceutical dependency is just one of the many facets of this loss of industrial capacity (Kota & Mahoney 2020: 1). It was argued that thanks to the delocalization of western industries, China was able to develop "unsurpassed ecosystems of industrial production encompassing the entire value chain from raw materials to final product", managing to "scale complex product designs into efficient mass production" (*ibid*.: 4). Perhaps, an amazing example of this dynamic can be found in the production of Apple's iPhone, allegedly the most recognizable item "made in the USA". In 2012 the *New York Times* reported on a dinner of "Silicon Valley's top luminaries" attended by Steve Jobs – Apple's boss – and President Obama where during Jobs's address Obama asked what it would take to re-shore the production of "almost 70 million iPhones, 30 million iPads and 59 million other products" that Apple sold in 2011 in the United States. Apple's chief answered that "[t]hose jobs aren't coming back", while other Apple's executive explained that this was not only about cheap labour, but also about "the vast scale of overseas factories as well as the flexibility, diligence and industrial skills of foreign workers" (Duhigg & Bradsher 2012). In two words: industrial capacity. It is also due to these dynamics that "the trade deficit with China has displaced 3.7 million jobs since 2001" (Kota & Mahoney 2020: 5).

Deindustrialization in the West has been a source of China's strategic advantage with regard to rare earth metals (REM). At the time of writing, China hosts most of the world's processing capacity and supplied 80 per cent of REM imported by the United States from 2014 to 2017. In 2017, China accounted for 81 per cent of the world's REM production, according to data from the US Geological Survey (Reuters Staff 2019). Until the 1990s the United States had a relatively significant output. In the 1990s, China decided to securitize this good, declaring rare-earth elements (REE) a "protected and strategic mineral" (Kalantzakos 2018: 119). The PRC possesses the largest and most valuable reserve in the world located in Bayan Obo, a mining site in the west of Inner Mongolia which in 2005 "accounted for 47 percent of the total rare-earth production of China, and 45 percent of that of the world" (*ibid.*). During that decade, China's production and export grew so fast that competitors in other countries were either put "out of business" or had to slow production (*ibid.*). As China started to sell REE at a low price, the mining industry in the US could no longer justify continuing operations. As western and US mining companies were shutting down, the PRC "sought effective ways to increase centralized control over the industry" (*ibid.*).

As was often the case, the US government facilitated China's rise. Indeed, in her book, Kalantzakos told the story of General Motors-owned Magnequench, which possessed a patent for neodymium-iron-boron (NdFeB) magnet. In 1995 it was bought by a joint venture of two Chinese groups with a US investment firm. Rather than imposing more stringent rules, the US administration approved the acquisition provided that Magnequench remained in the US "for at least five years"; one day after the deadline expired, the company shut its operations in the US and was moved to the PRC while American workers were laid off (*ibid.*: 120–1).

As it was rightly pointed out, this was a "strategic mistake" because "when the business left, so did the technology"; if in 1998 "90 percent of the world's magnet production was in the West – US, Europe, Japan – in a decade the balance of economic production shifted" (*ibid.*). This led to a domination by China that Kalantzakos described as "unparalleled in the previous history of strategic materials" (*ibid.*: 1).

Does this all matter and if so, why? Rare metals are used for production of an array of goods widely employed in modern societies, from electric and hybrid vehicles' batteries to computers; from wind turbines to superconductors; from jet engines, missile guidance systems to satellites and lasers. For instance, the British company BAE Systems, which will be involved in the delivery of nuclear-powered submarines in the context of the AUKUS (Australia, UK, US) deal, relies on REM to produce armaments. The same goes for Raytheon Company, a defence technology company, and Lockheed Martin Corporation (Reuters Staff 2019). In 2010, as Beijing was involved in a political dispute with Tokyo, it restricted the export of REE to Japan, an act that made some western countries rethink their REE strategy. As prices skyrocketed, the US, together with Australia, Russia and others, restarted or increased their REE production.

CHINA'S ECONOMIC WEAKNESSES VIS-À-VIS THE WEST

In recent years, we have often been reminded by scholars and commentators about Napoleon Bonaparte's prophecy on China shaking the world when it awakes. While it is still too early to determine whether the twenty-first century will become China's, certainly the 2010s were China's decade. Nonetheless, the PRC's immense international economic success remains an unaccomplished puzzle with clusters of pieces disorderly spread across the international board. One obvious and important area of foreign economic policy where this statement can be tested is that of multinational corporations. In 2016, David Shambaugh asked "[h]ow many Chinese corporations can you name? Most likely fewer than ten, or even five" (Shambaugh 2016: 139).

It would be an interesting exercise to stop ordinary people in the street and ask them the same question. At first glance, I could probably only name Huawei and Lenovo, perhaps the beer Tsingtao – if that qualifies as a multinational corporation. Alibaba and TikTok figure among the top Chinese businesses selling in tens of countries around the world, although one might point out that these are online platforms. This is not surprising; the Best Global Brands 2020 ranking, published by Interbrand, measures the degree of soft power wielded by multinational corporations (i.e., how well-known and respected a certain company is among the public). This ranking included only one Chinese company in the top one hundred, Huawei, which was placed 80th (Best Global Brands 2020). Huawei currently remains the only truly multinational Chinese company, especially from a logistical point of view. According to Shambaugh, if China lacks companies that are capable of operating globally this depends on several factors, including the substantially greater difficulty at competing abroad compared to the home market, in addition to lack of multicultural management and integration into western business culture, politicization, and vertical hierarchy among other things (Shambaugh 2016: 129–42).

From a different angle, one can see that Chinese companies have made progress, but they lag behind US, European, Japanese and South Korean companies. In 2021 the number of Chinese firms engaged in international economic operations increased by 16 per cent. Most interestingly, 111 firms from mainland China and Hong Kong made it into the 2018 Global Fortune 500, falling short of the number of US companies by just 15. However, it was reported that even when looking at Chinese so-called global firms "less than 20 percent of revenue comes from overseas" (McKinsey Global Institute 2019: 65–6). To take an example, a sector in which one might think Chinese companies are world leaders, such as smart phones, Chinese producers control 85 per cent of the Chinese market, and yet they only control 25 per cent of the global share, and between 35 and 50 per cent when it comes to first-tier components. On another note, McKinsey argued that the penetration of western MNCs in Chinese consumer markets is almost double the Chinese penetration in US markets – but western MNCs are losing ground (*ibid.*: viii).

This sends two messages: China provides such a huge market that some Chinese companies can afford not to become a leader in international markets. In a way, this is a strength, because it means they do not have to depend on foreign markets. But also it signals that these companies have not been able to beat competition in important economic areas. There are several technologies such as electric vehicles, smart phones, solar panels, robotics and cloud services, among others, where Chinese companies dominate the domestic market, performing poorly or with limited success on the global stage, while doing a good job at providing first-tier components (although China is making fast progress in smart phones, with the success of Xiaomi and with Transsion having become the leading manufacturer for sales in Africa) (*ibid.*: 65; Maina 2017).

Semiconductors, however, are China's technological Achilles' heel. Chinese companies are not influential players in this market – neither domestically nor internationally – including when it comes to first-tier components. According to McKinsey this "is not surprising", because in this sector the "technology barrier is extremely high": while producing an LCD requires only "11 process steps ... it takes about 500 steps to create a 20 nm chip in a foundry environment, but 1,500 steps for a 7 nm chip" (*ibid.*: 80). Based on the historical experience of countries such as Japan, South Korea, Taiwan and China itself, it was noted that it might take more than ten years for any given country to catch up with a certain technology once the government has assigned a strategic plan. Of the ingredients necessary for achieving this, China currently enjoys large-scale investments and access to a huge market, but it struggles when it comes to the acquisition of technology from abroad and an entrepreneurial environment that encourages competition and innovation – even though the Chinese state is proactive when it comes to stimulating investments and facilitating synergies (*ibid.*; Lee 2018: 4).

Finally, the McKinsey Global Institute's study noted that the exposure of economies to China has increased, but this has not systemically undermined the fundamentals of major economies. It is the developing world that is becoming increasingly tied into the Chinese economy. In fact, in the biggest economies such as those of Europe and North America "[e]xports to China typically account for less than 5 percent of gross output, and imports from China account for less than 5 percent of domestic consumption. Furthermore, Chinese FDI was equivalent to less than 1 percent of domestic investment" (*ibid.*: 6). Instead, countries with regional proximity, significant trade in resources and cross-border capital flows are most exposed to China. This suggests that while the

PRC is far from being able to coerce the US, Germany or Japan, it is succeeding among developing countries, mostly located in Asia and Africa. It must be said that while this does not have a direct impact on the above-mentioned states, in the long term it risks eroding their global influence.

The advantage that the West enjoys over China is not guaranteed forever – this was one of the lessons from Chapter 1 – especially if deeper political supervision of certain economic sectors is not applied. In 2013 Shambaugh maintained that China's exports were "still dominated by generally low-end consumer products" (Shambaugh 2013: 124). However, China has been moving fast since then. The *Financial Times* reported that in medium-level technology – such as electrical machinery – China is a "threat to industry in the US and other developed economies", while between 2007 and 2017 China's technology exports have made substantial gains, doubling their share of global exports (Hancock 2018). In Europe, there has been widespread concern about China's ownership of European strategic assets and companies. On the one hand, a third of the European bloc's total assets are now in the hands of foreign companies, and Chinese ownership amounts to 9.5 per cent of this third, not of the totality of European assets; from this viewpoint, the amount of Chinese ownership appears to be small (Reality Check Team 2019). On the other hand, some might find the trend concerning. Indeed, between 2007 and 2019 Chinese ownership increased in the last ten years from 2.5 to 9.5 per cent while, for instance, United States and Canadian interests decreased from 42 to 29 per cent; in addition, Chinese investments in the EU reached a record $36.5 billion in 2016, about 4 per cent of total foreign direct investment (FDI) stock in the EU (*ibid.*).

The main lesson from this seems to be that China does not dominate in western economies, although it has growing influence over them. Frenzy about Chinese economic operations and alarmist narratives are not justified. Yet, China's quasi-monopolistic power in a few sensitive industrial sectors and a fast-growing trend of Chinese investments in the West demand not only greater attention but also national coordination between different agencies and coalitions of like-minded states.

DECOUPLING AND THE RETURN OF
WHOLE-OF-GOVERNMENT IN THE WEST

This brief survey of those knotty areas, where the interdependence between China and several western countries can be problematic and can hide strategic risks, leads to an ambitious question: is it possible to decouple from China? A question that was brought to the fore by Donald Trump and his trade war on Beijing, it is an option that remains on the agenda of some countries and industries. Some refer to an economic separation and a technological one. Economic decoupling entails "the shrinking volume of imports and exports between both countries and gradually declining dependence on each other's market" (Wei 2019: 548–9). To some degree, this has already happened during and following the trade war between Washington and Beijing. Meanwhile, technological decoupling involves "the reduction in technological cooperation between the two countries and a decline of technological products in their trade volume" in addition to a decrease in "technology-related investments in each other's markets", and even here there are those who believe that to an extent decoupling "is already happening" (*ibid.*).

Can anyone decouple from China, then? It depends on the extent of decoupling. The Henry Jackson Society (HJS), among the most anti-China think tanks, acknowledged that the intelligence alliance of Five Eyes (FVEY) – formed by US, UK, Canada, Australia and New Zealand – "may not be able to regenerate self-sufficiency across all strategic sectors" – and certainly not even across non-sensitive industries (Rogers *et al.* 2020: 35). This is a sort of "negative decoupling", which de facto implies restrictions to, and sanctions on Chinese investments in sensitive areas. However, as the HJS noted, decoupling would be more effective if "each of the five powers" agreed to implement these measures in a coordinated manner. Indeed, one of the strengths of China's economic strategy is that it can divide and rule, if needed, by threatening to stop importing certain goods (Rogers *et al.* 2020: 34–6). Therefore, FVEY members should accept limited dependency on China in some strategic areas and commit to "forcing breakthroughs in frontier technologies that China does not yet dominate, rather than chasing after China's production of existing products" (*ibid.*: 36). This has been called "positive decoupling", a phrase which captures well the essence of

President Biden's Build Back Better World (B3W) project, discussed in Chapter 5. A third variant is "cooperative decoupling", which implies an extension of mutual intelligence cooperation "into wider spheres, where shared fiscal and economic cultures exist" (*ibid.*: 37). But as one can see, in any strategy for national decoupling from China, coalition-building is key because this is the only chance to mitigate the implications of not trading with such an economic giant like China.

Nonetheless, decoupling in an era of globalized supply chains is challenging, as a significant percentage of US imports from China involves US suppliers; indeed, a large part of Chinese exports to the US is dominated by foreign invested enterprises (FIE). These sectors have been severely hit by the trade war. Therefore, decoupling will upset US companies as much as businesses from American allies, especially since the inflow of FDIs in China is second in the world with $187 billion (World Bank 2021). It also varies by industry. Some might be able to decouple but for others it will be almost impossible without impacting profits. Shehzad H. Qazi, managing director of the China Beige Book, a platform that analyses data on China's economy for investors, wisely admitted that "companies are going to be incredibly resistant to anything that hurts their share price", and they would need "tax incentives" to make any shift "palatable" (Johnson & Gramer 2020). The economist Douglas Irwin has warned that current socio-economic turmoil in capitalist democracies may facilitate decoupling. But, drawing a parallel with the interwar period, he noted that "[w]hen some countries go down this road, it forces other countries to go down this road as well, ... So these things can spiral – that's certainly the story of the 1930s" (*ibid.*). For the time being, therefore, one can cautiously state that "[s]ome disentanglement is, of course, appropriate" and "selective, considered decoupling might enhance US competitiveness" but it will have to be a fine-grained one (Wyne 2020: 57). For reasons articulated in Chapter 2, the US struggles to have a coherent stance on decoupling, and a perfect solution in a world order split between economic and security interests is not possible. This has emerged clearly through different important government statements. Biden's US trade representative Katherine Tai on the same day stated that there is "no point in talking about decoupling", and that to slow down China's "rate of innovation" the US needs to work closely with non-Chinese allies, clearly contradicting herself (Lewis 2021). US senator Chris Coon, instead, argued that the US should build "a high fence around a small yard of our ... crown jewels of technology" while "strik[ing] the right balance to avoid ... decoupling of global tech industries between the United States and China" (Coons 2019).

A point worth noting, however, is that while the attention is on whether countries like the US, Australia, Japan or the EU can decouple from China, we may overlook two aspects. First we should not assume that it is only these countries that are exploring decoupling options. There is a belief among a group of Chinese scholars that the Chinese themselves might be able to partially decouple from the West through a dual circulation strategy, that is, leveraging on its expanding domestic market – an asset other countries lack – and on increasing trade with other countries (Wei 2019: 550–3). Indeed, in a context of "weaponized interdependence", it has been argued that states that are unable to shape networks in a favourable manner "may attempt to isolate themselves" (Farrell & Newman 2021: 50). However, a different group of Chinese observers have acknowledged that this could halt the pace of innovation in China, in addition to other economic implications (Wei 2019: 550–53).

Secondly, the Covid-19 global pandemic, which has already had a major impact on the slowdown or disruption of supply chains, could be the enabler of decoupling, which is seen as a solution to regain resilience and overcome vulnerabilities. However, if this is the case in the short term it will come at a high cost for consumers, especially since it would happen in an almost uncontrolled fashion, which means governments may not be able to decide what, when, and to what extent they decouple.

While decoupling might seem a temporary, extemporaneous and reactive measure, some governments have questioned the benefits of neoliberalism – responsible for many strategic failures over the last three decades – and have looked into the possibility of a more integrated approach to policy-making, especially with regards to China. Concepts like cross-government, pan-government, whole-of-government and whole-of-society have entered the political agenda in the US and other western countries. Not only has this been a reaction dictated by security concerns – as illustrated in the following chapter: the West, I argue, could not neglect the fact that China's whole-of-government approach to policy has had its benefits. As Kerry Brown has said, there is a huge irony in the fact that the leading capitalist economy in the world is going to be ruled by a communist party. Similarly, Hugh White explained that "[t]here is not just one political model for economic success", and if one compares "Georgian Britain, mid-nineteenth century America, Bismarck's Germany, Meiji Japan and Lee Kwan Yew's Singapore", one can see that "[t]he differences are at least as striking as the similarities" (White 2013: 35). The economist Branko Milanovic explained in *Foreign Affairs* that China's positive performance has "undermine[ed] the West's claim that there is a necessary link between capitalism and liberal democracy" (Milanovic 2020: 12). In the context of the global supply chain disruption caused by Covid-19, this led the patently liberal magazine, *The Economist*, to comment that one of the lessons of Covid-19 in relation to China's position within global supply chains, is that "change would involve upending well-established political and economic theories" (2020).

In conclusion, it is difficult to determine whether decoupling is possible and how far western governments dare to challenge one of their ideological pillars, namely globalization, that has endured for almost 80 years. Yet, as Covid-19 raised questions of western over-reliance on China in some areas, analysts and governments have started to reconsider the relationship between political power and the free market. This is a long-overdue move and the hope is that these policies will compel governments to tame markets more than they were able to do in the past 30 years. To an extent, this marks a success for China, because implementing a whole-of-government and whole-of-society approach in the West is an acknowledgement that the Chinese model – much criticized on the grounds of ideology and values – has its benefits. Furthermore, greater centralization of powers could lead to the erosion of democratic space and to diffused, unofficial forms of authoritarianism in the West, which is still strangled by financial recession. However, this shift is also a major problem for the PRC, because it increases the political obstacles that China will encounter when operating in western countries. Increased control of strategic industries in the West will require greater effort from China to shape the LIO and its geoeconomics networks to its advantage for the sake of national interests.

4

The dilemmas of China's engagement with the world

"If China wants to be the new global standard, how can it stay special?"

Philipp Renninger

In reflecting on the strategic mistakes of the West in its relationship with the PRC, we have observed that these flaws originated from short-sighted policies, but also from the fact that China, for the West, poses an economy-security dilemma. The West's delay in coming to this realization has led to the erosion of the LIO. In the following chapter, I focus on the conundrum facing China that has arisen from the intensification of its relationship with the outside world. Indeed, the LIO is not only a source of dilemma for the West in the face of a rising China, but it has become a source of tension for China itself. Capturing opportunities abroad requires opening the national economy to global capitalism. Yet, deeper integration with the global order will make the PRC's borders more porous to American, European and South Korean businesses, and to western ideas more generally. This threatens to undermine the internal political and cultural hegemony of the Chinese Communist Party, which will have to scrutinize and, if necessary, restrict China's engagement with the world. The PRC elite will have to carefully weigh up whether they want to expand or retrench from certain international commitments, whether this means convincing different foreign constituencies that Beijing is keen to fight climate change and the environmental crisis; or deciding the extent to which China's military power should be employed abroad. It is unlikely that the CCP will find an answer to these dilemmas any time soon, and China's rise as a global power could make it more difficult to work out a coherent path.

DOES CHINA WANT TO DISMANTLE THE LIBERAL ORDER?

The journal *International Organization* celebrated its 75th anniversary in the spring of 2021 with a special issue dedicated to the LIO. The journal and the LIO came into being at roughly the same time. In the opening article, the authors asked whether the rise of China is "a fundamental challenge to the LIO, or has the country been sufficiently co-opted into the order that it is now a 'responsible stakeholder'?" (Lake *et al.* 2021: 241). This is a worthwhile question because the socio-political hybridity that characterizes the PRC has implications for how China integrates with or detaches from the LIO. China "is not a democracy and shows no tendencies toward democratization", while it is "comfortable with the underlying Westphalian values of sovereignty and noninterference" (*ibid.*: 241–2). However, it "has joined the major multilateral IOs, benefited in tremendous ways from these memberships, and even replicated at least the form of these" (*ibid.*). Along similar lines, many other scholars ask whether the PRC is a "status quo power" or a "revisionist power" aiming at "within-system change" or "fundamental change"; a "rule-breaker" as opposed to a state "reliant on the predictability and benign stability of the global political and economic order"; an "order breaking" player as opposed to an "order upholding" one (Nathan 2016: 165; Brown 2017: 7; Rapp-Hooper *et al.* 2019).

Andrew J. Nathan has argued that since China joined the LIO it "worked to influence the way in which regimes have continued to evolve" (Nathan 2016: 165–6). To some extent, China's rise to economic and military great power has disrupted the LIO, because the latter, to function, has always needed an organizing hegemon like the United States. The LIO embodies American power and American power embodies the LIO. The very fact that China is involuntarily changing the balance of power is a disruptive process. Taking this into account, Nathan's idea that the LIO "is resilient" vis-à-vis the rise of China is problematic; a LIO not led by the US, which is declining, will be something different, even if China "prefers to join it rather than to overturn it" (*ibid.*: 168).

The issue of balance of power is critical because it will allow China to shape international regimes' rules. Indeed, Amitav Acharya noted that we should not assume that "just because China, India, and other rising powers have benefitted from the liberal hegemonic order, they will abide by its norms and institutions", as they might "alter" its structure (Acharya 2014: 50). Similarly, White noted that even if China does not appear to pursue international "leadership" this does not equal "reluctance to exercise power in pursuit of its own agenda" (White 2013: 45–6). A policy brief from Carnegie Endowment for International Peace maintained, instead, that China's behaviour is "far more complex" than what black-and-white views can possibly offer, and difficult to put a label on at this stage (Rapp-Hooper *et al.* 2019).

My answer to the question of whether China is a "challenge" to the LIO or a "co-opted" country is that it is both. However, far from hiding behind academic ambiguity, I argue that there is a less ambivalent answer. The PRC's approach to the LIO is one of selective globalism: China is cherry-picking. It welcomes whatever does not threaten its core industries, culture or political system, and what it can best influence and dominate. Yet, it rejects what it perceives as a threat or what its companies struggle to compete with. Although it sounds unusual to westerners, China is a meticulous interpreter of sovereignty and national interests. The fact that some countries in the West have diluted their sovereignty makes China's behaviour so surprising to many people. In other words, China, like other great powers, "naturally seeks to maximize its ability to shape its international environment to the extent it is capable" (Norris 2016: 55). However, while it has not decided what relationship it will have with the future world order, "for the time being it seeks to maintain as unconstrained an environment as possible" – both geostrategically in the Asia-Pacific and politically within the institutions of the LIO (*ibid.*). In the choices China makes, it will have "core interests" over which it does not intend to negotiate – like territorial claims over the South China Sea – and secondary interests – about which Beijing is more indulgent – as with everything that is not a core interest.

What is China's view of this? To a certain extent, it is not possible to provide a precise answer to this question because the PRC is not a monolith from an institutional point of view; nuances if not differences always exist even in authoritarian countries. Alison Kaufman from the

CAN Corporation singled out three perspectives with regard to Chinese perceptions of the international system (IS). All of them build on the assumption that the IS remains essentially as it was in the nineteenth century: powerful states vying for the domination of weak states. However, perspectives differ over the extent to which China should engage with the IS. One view, informed by the history of the Century of Humiliation, believes that the IS remains biased because it is constructed around western rules and interests to "subjugate" weaker nations therefore China's role in it should be limited (Kaufman 2010: 12–16). A second perspective maintains that China should pursue "a central role" in today's IS in order to shape rules of the LIO (*ibid.*, 16–22). A third, more audacious view advocates for China to become "a framer of international rules" to change the IS according to Beijing's national interests or even to overcome the current IS by founding "a new international system superior to the current one" (*ibid.*: 23–6).

Since the beginning of the Xi Jinping era, the third view has become more prominent. However, because foreign policy is a compromise between different domestic schools of thought and international pressures, China's engagement with the LIO will remain multifaceted for some time. But there is no doubt that as the PRC grows more powerful it will advocate more strongly for changing the rules of the game. This intention has been clearly spelled out in different official documents, and the Chinese elite do not shy away from this message when they engage in diplomacy. In 2015, at the Rose Garden of the White House, Xi Jinping told Obama that China wants a "new model of major-country relationship". Xi's words implying that China should have greater leverage over the rules of international regimes – from trade to seabed issues, from domestic political economy to human rights. Likewise, in 2017 the heads of state of the BRICS group – which includes China – advocated for "a more just, equitable, fair, democratic and representative international political and economic order" (BRICS Leaders Xiamen Declaration 2017: 1).

Perhaps one can infer from this discussion that there is no answer yet to how and to what extent the PRC will pursue integration as opposed to revolution in the LIO; nevertheless, the implications of China's challenge already reverberate across the world order. Indeed, even if China might be far from winning this game – although, can anybody really win, especially alone? – the global balance of power has already shaken the architecture of the LIO; by favouring a shift towards multipolarity, it has undermined the political resolve of multilateral institutions. For instance, over the past two decades the WTO has struggled to implement its agenda since the international leadership of the United States has weakened, while emerging powers advocate for reforming the institution. But the more China and other powers rise, the more challenging it is to achieve a plural agreement on how multilateral institutions should be reformed. The WTO, indeed, is in worse shape than ever and as explained in a report from Chatham House, it "faces a make-or-break moment" (Schneider-Petsinger 2020). Inside the WTO, China continues to play a smart game as the standard bearer of developing countries. Indeed, there is still no agreed definition of what constitutes a developed or developing country at the WTO, and states can self-determine their status. China, despite being the second biggest economy in the world, defines itself as "developing" and it has taken advantage of this status. In April 2019, when the US was attempting to restrict the number of "developing" countries that receive preferential treatment, China went on the diplomatic offensive. Consistent with a strategy of selective globalism, the commerce ministry's spokesman Gao Feng stated that: while "[w]e do not shy away from our international responsibilities", the PRC will "assume obligations in the WTO that are compatible with our own economic development level and capabilities" (quoted in Zhou 2019).

Regardless of how different China's world order will be, we are already witnessing a clash between two irreconcilable truths. The United States and other countries in the West are right to demand that China complies with WTO rules. China, with its selective globalism, has taken advantage and there has been a legitimate backlash against its modus operandi. However, as China notes, the LIO is based on an international regime of rules, values and standards that have been imposed in the interest of the United States. If both positions are valid, there is a risk that who has the greater power will determine who is right and who is wrong, as is often the case in history. The next chapter will reflect on whether we are in a new Cold War. In the meantime, China's hesitation to pursue further integration within the LIO and to take greater international responsibilities reveals that even Beijing is faced with structural dilemmas.

CHINA'S DOMESTIC CONUNDRUM: BETWEEN ECONOMIC GROWTH AND POLITICAL STABILITY

In early September 2021, the nationalist blogger Li Guangman wrote that China is in the middle of "a profound revolution" that is taking the CCP to its "original mission ... to the essence of socialism" (quoted in Tang 2021). Li described celebrities involved in scandals as "social tumours" (*ibid.*). His article was cited by several state-controlled media outlets, giving the impression it was backed by the CCP (Mai & Rui 2021). At around the same time, it was reported that television talent shows similar to *American Idol* "featuring men deemed too effeminate" were outlawed (Kuo 2021). Similarly, it was said that one of the richest actresses in China, Zhao Wei, was de facto "cancelled" online (*ibid.*). Too often in the West such events are attributed to China's authoritarian, if not totalitarian, regime. However, this fails to capture the logic that lies behind certain actions. The PRC is governed through a nationalist political system that closely supervises economic and societal activities in the name of national interest, such as increasing geopolitical power and strengthening the role of the ruling party. Not only is this an issue for the US and other trade partners of China – for reasons discussed in Chapter 2 – it is also a problem for China itself. While the PRC has benefited from state interventionism, if it wants to influence the rest of the world it will have to expose itself more to foreign economic and cultural actors and ideas. The Chinese economy continues to rely on a strong mercantilist component, and it is under pressure to engage more with the global economy. Yet, the PRC elite are keen to pursue this endeavour on their own terms; they want to avoid an erosion of the CCP's legitimacy and influence. Jonathan Fenby observed that "openness has always been regarded as dangerous, by emperors of the past and today's Communist Party alike" (Fenby 2017: 31). Similarly, talking about Prince Gong's reflections in the aftermath of the Second Opium War (1856–60), Henry Kissinger asked "can a society maintain its cohesion while seeming to adapt to the conqueror?" (2011: 70). Openness and isolation always have their pros and cons. For Fenby, however, today "[s]elf-preservation of this kind comes at a heavy cost" (2017: 32). Deng Xiaoping, in fact, famously warned that "[i]f you open the window for fresh air, you have to expect some flies to blow in".

This dilemma influences Xi Jinping's actions. Kerry Brown notes that "[t]he outside world is a theatre of opportunity, but China must resist some aspects of it" (2017: 205). This is why, he added, "foreign interests have taken a battering" in China since Xi (*ibid.*: 207). Building on the Century of Humiliation narrative, the underlining message from Xi Jinping is that China is not a land of "limitless opportunity for profits" from where one can walk away "scot-free" (*ibid.*: 208). One of the priorities in Xi's domestic agenda, as Elizabeth Economy pointed out, has been that of making the PRC's borders "selectively permeable" by filtering ideas and capital through "regulatory, legal, and technological impediments", while increasing what goes out of China (Economy 2018: 11). To her, this is a "long game" in which the Chinese elite demonstrate their preference for "control rather than competition" and accept economic outcomes that might be "suboptimal in the near term" but that can have "longer strategic value" (*ibid.*: 15). For instance, restrictions to the internet constrain research and innovation by slowing the internationalization of Chinese scientific research and ideas (*ibid.*: 89), however, it also allows the PRC to filter ideological threats and to protect its technological champions.

Pundits have linked Xi Jinping's nationalist domestic policies to the Communiqué on the Current State of the Ideological Sphere, commonly referred to as Document no. 9, released in April 2013 by the CCP. The document denounced efforts to "gouge an opening through which to infiltrate our ideology" and warned about a series of political "perils", including "constitutionalism", "civil society", "universal values", and the promotion of "the West's view of media" (ChinaFile 2013). Yet, it was between 2020 and 2021 that Xi Jinping gave the world a clear taste of all this by further tightening the nationalist straitjacket. In November 2020, the government prevented Alibaba's Ant Group from listing on the stock exchanges of Shanghai and Hong Kong. Subsequently, it limited the maximum time Chinese children could play video games to three hours per day; it launched a crackdown on celebrities – they should not be idolized by citizens; and made moves against cram schools. In addition, in the summer of 2021 several for-profit private tutoring companies were expropriated by the state, while stricter rules on the private insurance industry were imposed at a time when just 5 per cent of the country's 1.4 billion population had insurance. Even the drinking culture came under the scrutiny of the authorities.

This set of implementations come under the framework of Common Prosperity. What this intends to achieve is contested. Xi Jinping presented it as a policy that would narrow the gap between rich and poor in China, which is instrumental to the legitimacy of the party and to the underlining pragmatic Marxism adopted by the CCP. Yet, one wonders whether this policy provides the party with additional opportunities to rein in influential players that, as they grow bigger, might become too powerful even for the CCP. Indeed, Common Prosperity has also been described as a "hard pivot toward asserting greater state control of society and the economy" (Hass 2021).

Although one could easily describe this politics as dictatorial, that might be a superficial way of looking at it. It is certainly an example of authoritarianism. However, constraining the power of tech giants and regulating the private tutoring sectors is necessary for the CCP to preserve the Chinese-ness of the PRC or, in other words, to grow capitalistically while safeguarding national sovereignty. From another perspective, it might be seen simply as an effort by the Chinese elite – albeit in a spectacular way – to correct the "excesses" of Deng Xiaoping's reformist agenda, captured by the phrase "let some people get rich first". Indeed, the state-run newspaper *Economic Daily* reported that the crackdown is a "short-term cost for healthy long-term growth". In addition, as Fenby noted, when the PRC elite launched the reforms in 1978, "the old ways had lost credibility and there was a hunger for experimentation of a different kind from Mao's adventurism" (2017: 56). Today, instead, Xi can emphasize the "contribution of the first three decades of Communist rule to the country's renaissance" (*ibid.*).

The million-dollar question is how long China will be able to grow at the desired pace, while being so restrictive vis-à-vis foreign flows? Any forecast on the resilience of Sino-capitalism here would be risky since too many times predictions – and hopes – about China have turned out to be wrong. Although it seems predestined to overtake the US economy soon, that does not necessarily mean that each of its challenges will be resolved. One might look to different areas for answers about the future of China's political economy and domestic governance. In the West, an economic crisis is believed to be the potential trigger for systemic change in China, for instance, many feared or wished for this scenario in late 2021 when Evergrande, a major Chinese real estate entity, was the most indebted company in the world. What seems a more reliable indicator is the mood among the younger Chinese generations. Will they demand more democracy? It has often been taken for granted that they would, but there remains too much uncertainty about this today. As *The Times* suggested, China has 400 million millennials who are happy to trade democracy for the iPhone (Sherwell 2020). Meanwhile, an *Economist* special report on young Chinese citizens in their twenties pointed out that although young Chinese people "speak out for social causes", "increasingly youths do not question the regime's claim that loving country and party are one and the same" (*The Economist* 2021). Others have pointed out that the younger generations are not more internationalist than the older ones, and they still express a lot of nationalism. The lesson from this and from the past is that one should not expect any change to China's domestic politics and society for the foreseeable future.

STRONG OR WEAK POWER? CHINA'S MILITARY APPROACH

The economic rise of the PRC has led to a massive increase in defence expenditure over the past 20 years or so. Yet, as with everything else, China's military strategy is ambiguous and constantly evolving. Indeed, the way China manages its military affairs appears to be influenced by a desire to act below the threshold of war, applying deception and using economic levers to coerce the adversary as opposed to military power. Yet, in parallel to this there are trends showing that China is preparing to become a military power. Making sense of this contradiction makes the job of the western policy-maker even more difficult.

This ambiguity begs the question as to whether one should look at China through the lens of the Sinologist or through that of the international relations scholar. That is, is there anything specifically Chinese about the rise of China and its military strategy? Or, is this just another great power that will behave in IR terms like its predecessors – like the Spanish, Dutch and British empire or the US hegemony, among others? This divide can polarize discussions about China, but there are good arguments to be made on both sides. The military strategy of the PRC continues to be informed by Marxism and Sun Tzu. This has tangible implications. Marxism was imported by Mao into China, filtered through the slogan "seek truth from facts" – a phrase originating from an ancient Chinese book – denoting the pragmatic application of theory, which needs to derive from and be for the real world. This is important because Chinese strategy-makers, in theory, act based on real material conditions rather than on ideological principles and predetermined goals, such as wars intended to export democracy. This is something, according to William Whitson, that "Westerners do not understand ... because they think victory comes to those with the most destructive weapons and through the application of Courses of Action (CoAs)" (Thomas 2014: 45). Furthermore, if a military strategy is carefully based on a realistic assessment of threats and opportunities, it means that this will evolve together with changing circumstances.

Although this materialist component is clearly related to Marxism, it also resembles features of the millenary military tradition of General Sun Tzu, who prioritized caution and emphasized the importance of intelligence gathering. Among the most famous citations of Tzu one finds: "he will win who knows when to fight and when not to fight", a phrase that highlights the centrality of intelligence and warns against the risks of ideologically-driven military adventures; "in the midst of chaos, there is also opportunity", which emphasizes the importance of deception; and "victorious warriors win first and then go to war", which demands a careful assessment of strengths and weaknesses on both side of the battlefield prior to engaging in conflict. In more practical terms, this is translated by the PRC into ideas such as active defence and grey zone warfare (GZW). Active defence is a principle that has been central to China's military strategy since Mao. It has evolved several times, but in general it entails a mixture of pre-emptive and offensive measures of strategic defence in combination with offensive action at the operational and tactical levels. De facto, this means, as China says, that on a high scale "[w]e will not attack unless we are attacked, but we will surely counterattack if attacked", while at a tactical level assertive actions can be taken to strengthen China's position (Office of the Secretary of Defense 2021: 33–4). The PRC's 2019 Defence White Paper reaffirmed active defence as the basis for its military strategy (State Council 2019: 8–9).

Within this framework the idea of GZW, a conceptual development compared to the better known "hybrid warfare", makes more sense.

While one cannot put a straitjacket on the definition of GZW, nevertheless, it tends to be conducted through acts of incremental aggression that go beyond ordinary or peacetime competition but that, at the same time, remain below the (subjective) threshold of war. The long-term objective of GZW operations is one of gradually eroding the operational advantage of a rival state while avoiding the risk of direct confrontation which may be difficult to sustain. This approach has been central to how China's military operate in contested islands in the South China Sea and East China Sea or near Taiwan.

However, perhaps due to its integration with the West, China has also learned from other giants of strategic thinking, such as Carl von Clausewitz and, above all, Alfred Mahan. China has been preparing for active warfare. It has done this in two ways. After starting a process of modernization in the post-Cold War years – driven by its threat assessment of the West – China has deprioritized its ground forces to invest technologically in its navy, air force and missiles. The People's Liberation Army Navy is key in this context. For contemporary Chinese military strategists, the "traditional mentality that land outweighs the sea must be abandoned, and great importance has to be attached to managing the seas and oceans and protecting maritime rights and interests" (State Council 2015: 6). The ascendancy of a naval force, capable of operating at a distance far from the homeland, has been a constant within empires and among great powers. China currently lacks the logistical forward base for projecting its military power overseas, although a new modern aircraft carrier and the naval base in Djibouti will help fill this gap.

As the navy expands its geographical scope, the People's Liberation Army (PLA) has developed powerful ballistic and cruise missiles capable of preventing adversaries from enjoying freedom of manoeuvre not only within the first island chain, but also – possibly – beyond that. In addition, the PLA development of a hypersonic missile capable of reaching speeds between Mach 5 and Mach 10 has not only surprised the rest of the world – which now has to catch up – but has also led pundits to wonder whether we are at the start of a new arms race. The story of the hypersonic missile – like China's investments in military uses of artificial intelligence – may not signal a military build-up; rather, it may reveal Beijing's attempt at leapfrogging into some niches that will allow China to compensate for weaknesses in its capabilities. This reflects the PRC's domestic economic policies, as China has sought since 1978 to skip stages of development. Yet, such a model leaves behind a degree of unevenness and unresolved limits that might one day become a problem.

Given all this, it might be asked what China wants to do with all this power. There is a spectrum of possibilities that depends on the context. Usually, when a state accumulates military power, it does so to gain respect in the international arena. Respect translates into greater leverage when negotiating diplomatic agreements, or more appeal when signalling resolve to allies or reassuring them, or in warning others that any foreign interference will incur the costs of deterrence. If one looks more specifically at modern Chinese history, these factors have driven both economic and military growth. This is also the case nowadays with China's stance on the South China Sea, where China needs to exploit its natural resources, support fishery – an industry of 10 million workers – and influence a highly strategic area for global trade. Beyond the first island chain, this power will remain limited for the foreseeable future and will be used to protect the trade of energy resources and foodstuffs coming from the Persian Gulf and Africa. The main focus will be in the Asia-Pacific, where China is most likely to become an assertive player, and because its power projection beyond that region is currently limited. Here, Beijing will want "to counter, co-opt, or circumvent what it perceives as excessive American influence around the Chinese periphery, while avoiding overt confrontation with the United States" (Gill 2007: 10).

But there are two reasons why China will also have to appear responsible if it does not want to scare neighbouring countries. First of all, the Pax Americana has shown that rule by coercion is not enough, and that consensus is a key ingredient for success. Secondly, China might want to have formal alliances itself one day. So far, Beijing has purposely avoided upgrading its partnerships to formal alliances; but another lesson from the quasi-global hegemony of the US is that there is no grand strategy worthy of this name without a network of alliances. If China really wanted to become a global power – something that concerns many in the West – it would have to begin building such a network. The unease at attempting to convince Russia to withdraw its troops from Ukraine in the spring of 2022, revealed that China sees future alliances emerging from outside the West.

In sum, China's military power confirms the hybrid character of the country, which cannot be reduced to any particular model. As Kissinger once noted, China's grand strategy is like the Chinese board game *wei qi*. China does not seek a decisive victory, as it would do if it were playing chess. Rather, it pursues "partially interlocking areas of strength", which means that the "winner is not always immediately obvious" (Kissinger 2011: 23). At a time when military institutions all over the world reflect on the importance of understanding the continuum between peace and war, that is, the grey zone, it seems relevant to emphasize that the chances for China embarking on a large-scale conflict are low, and that its growing military power will eventually be part of a comprehensive orchestration of the levers of power, especially economic ones. To an extent, this means the rest of the world can relax and should not be concerned about China's outright military interventions. The PRC is carefully building its strengths, aware of its weaknesses. Yet, as its power increases it will react more confidently whenever it feels its interests are undermined by the West.

CHINA'S CLIMATE CHANGE AGENDA AND PROSPECTS OF GREAT POWER COOPERATION

There are several examples that help us assess the depth, or lack, of engagement that the PRC has with the LIO. One of the most current and consequential issues is that of its commitment to combating climate change. This seems not only to be a problem of domestic economic security for China, more interestingly for this book, it has become a test of China's global leadership and responsibility, as climate change has become central to the international agenda. Furthermore, this issue promises to add an additional layer of complexity to the management of the great powers' relations.

As demonstrated by its engagement in the WTO, Beijing has confirmed a selective approach to the climate change agenda. It is willing to support multilateral agreements to the extent that environmental targets can be met on time and without undermining domestic interests. Until the Kyoto Protocol in 1997, the PRC "was not required to set emissions caps on any greenhouse gases" and avoiding "binding emissions caps was a vital factor in ratifying the treaty" for Beijing (Gong 2011: 159–60). Since the 1970s, China's posture on environmental policies was one of prioritizing domestic development. This posture has not substantially changed. After Kyoto, China's Position on the Copenhagen Climate Change Conference stated, among other principles, that there should be "differentiated responsibilities" between countries, meaning that developed countries continue to carry more responsibility because of "their historical cumulative emissions and current high per capita emissions" (National People's Congress 2009). A few years later, Beijing pledged to deliver on the objectives of the Paris Agreement in 2015, suggesting that it would have to make changes to its economy to keep global warming at 1.5°C (United Nations Framework Convention on Climate Change). Recently, however, the NGO Climate Action reported that China's policies have been "insufficient" to meet this target, although that does not mean this will not be met by 2030 and that there have not been positive steps to overcome the use of coal (Climate Action Tracker 2021). Given all this, it is not surprising that at the most recent Conference of Parties in Glasgow (COP26), China and India, leading the developing countries, managed to include in the final communiqué a promise to "phase down" rather than "phase out" usage of coal from their economies (Ellis-Petersen 2021). Although the whole world learned of this change when India's environment minister Bhupender Yadav read out the statement in tears, it was reported that China "pushed hard for a softening of the language over coal in the final negotiations" (*ibid.*). At the summit, a spokesperson for China's foreign ministry urged developed countries "to take the lead in stopping using coal" while explaining that for developing countries substituting traditional with sustainable ways of producing energy remains a challenge (Ni 2021). China has sought to buy precious time for its national industrial system to adapt to such a structural transition.

How should these developments be interpreted from a world order perspective? China's commitment to the climate change agenda is directly proportional to "other national priorities, especially if climate action can bring important benefits that would not otherwise obtain" (Harris 2011: 143). This might explain why China's stance towards climate change "appears difficult to comprehend", since, for instance, an "aggressive" attempt at reducing carbon has corresponded with a diplomatic commitment to oppose "cap[s] [to] its greenhouse gas emissions" (Moore 2011: 147). Ultimately, "domestic stability and economic growth" remain China's priority (*ibid.*: 157). This leads us to consider two aspects about China's relationship with the international order. First, it takes us back to an issue mentioned earlier in this book, that is, the tension between universal and national rights. Although per-person emissions in the PRC remain about half those of the US, overall China has been the most polluting country since 2006; currently, China alone is responsible for producing a quarter of all global greenhouse gases. This means that while China is asked to limit its emissions, Beijing can also blame global warming and pollution on US citizens. There is no easy answer to this dilemma.

Second, the PRC's strategic calculations in climate change negotiations highlight the continuing importance of Marxism in Chinese foreign policy narratives. As Domenico Losurdo noted, class struggle is "not restricted" to the clash between "bourgeoisie and proletariat, but includes in its very structure and articulation anti-colonial struggles against capitalist imperialism" (quoted in Boer 2021: 278). Although it was noted that anti-imperialism since the 1980s was partly replaced or at least complemented by "anti-hegemonism [*fandui baquanzhuyi*]" by the 1981 resolution of the CPC Central Committee, it seems that implicitly Marxism continues to feed the narrative about how China advocates for its rights and those of the rest of the developing world (*ibid.*: 175). When talking about anti-imperialism and anti-hegemonism, it is difficult not to see that the climate change agenda and the transition to the green economy intersects with relations between the two most prominent great powers, the United States and China, adding an additional layer of complexity – or more simply, just another excuse for arguing – to an increasingly comprehensive relationship. From a world order perspective, two more questions arise. First, is China seeking leadership in climate change diplomacy? If it has used climate change diplomacy to lead developing countries, it has not yet pursued global leadership on climate policy. Elizabeth Economy noted that leadership is "costly" as it would require of China more coherence and less ambiguity (2017). This was especially clear when Trump, de facto, "offered up" such leadership by withdrawing the US from the Paris Agreement (*ibid.*).

Second, will climate change policy become a space for the great powers' cooperation? One should not assume that the answer is "yes". In the field of international relations, liberal scholarship maintains that despite the world order being anarchic, institutions of global governance can facilitate the transparency and information necessary for cooperation between the great powers. Furthermore, it appears logical to think that when the survival of humanity is at stake – whether threatened by a financial crisis or by a pandemic – great powers might want to cooperate, because without cooperation there could be a higher price to pay. The latter will have negative implications for everyone. During the Cold War, for instance, the US and the USSR agreed on a progressive dismantling of a certain number of nuclear warheads. If the US and the USSR managed to do this during an era of heightened tensions, why should the US and China not manage to do the same?

There are some good reasons to believe that cooperation is not an obvious outcome. International security pundit Bruce Jones noted that at least until Covid-19 "there were good reasons to extrapolate from what had happened in earlier global crises that the major powers ... would put aside their growing geopolitical rivalry to manage shared global threats when it truly mattered" (Jones 2021: 1). Yet, what we have seen in recent years, with both Covid-19 and climate change, deserves some reflection. To begin with, while during the Cold War it was relatively easy to determine whether the USSR or the US were decreasing the number of nuclear warheads, establishing with accuracy whether China or the US will genuinely and diligently commit to a reduction of CO_2 or other pollutants is more challenging. Of course, this matter will be covered by a veil of ambiguity just thick enough to create mutual mistrust. The US and China might try to delegitimize each other in front of the international community or potential allies, accusing each other of not doing enough to save the world. Speaking of mistrust and delegitimization, the Covid-19 pandemic already showed us this type of eventuality, as both great powers were keen to blame one another for the origins of the virus. Donald Trump termed it the "Chinese virus", while China accused the US of fuelling conspiracy theories.

Another difference between the Cold War and today, is that at the time there were no tangible consequences for the state decreasing the number of nuclear warheads; and either way, each state continued to have enough nuclear warheads to command respect and deter the adversary. Instead, less production of CO_2 will mean a slowing down of the economy: countries will not be able to compensate until the right technology for exploiting energy in a sustainable way is available. This continues to be an issue for the Chinese economy but also for many developing countries that China seeks to represent in international summits.

Finally, the problem of acting against climate change intersects with the development of a green economy. Not only might this not benefit from the great powers' cooperation; it is also possible that such a shift will increase inter-imperial rivalry between the great powers in a grab of resources necessary for a green economy. This seems especially relevant in sectors such as electric cars and digital infrastructure, two areas that will form the so-called next-generation technologies and be a main pillar of the world economy. This will add pressure to some developing regions where China is particularly active, such as Central Africa and Latin America. The United Nations warned of two hotspots: "more than half of the world's lithium resources lies beneath the salt flats in the Andean regions of Argentina, Bolivia and Chile"; and "nearly 50% of world cobalt reserves are in the Democratic Republic of the Congo", which accounts for over two-thirds of global production of the mineral" (UNCTAD 2021).

It is hard not to be cynical, and one should consider that climate change, more than any other issue, is likely to see at least a degree of cooperation but unfortunately, it is just one of the several facets of contemporary Sino-American and Sino-western relations. These relations are currently experiencing more turmoil than they ever have in the past 50 years, as the next chapter shows. The co-existence of cooperative and competitive elements, and the strategic ambiguity that stems from them, has become a constant in the China policy of many western countries. This comes down to the fact that the LIO, despite being characterized by much interdependence, remains politically anarchic because it is fragmented into many territorial units.

Sino-western relations in the post-Trump era

"Is the world entering a new cold war? Our answer is yes and
no. Yes if we mean a protracted international rivalry ... No if
we mean the Cold War".

Hal Brands and John Lewis Gaddis

The first two chapters of this book sought to set the historical and institutional contexts which have facilitated the rise of the PRC, and that
have led to a complex relationship between the latter and the West. The
third and fourth chapters, however, have sought to flip the perspective
and to look at the challenges faced by China amidst growing engagement with a LIO dominated by the West. This final chapter looks at
recent events by providing an illustration of the conundrum faced by
some western countries in the making of their China policy. It shows
how dealing with the PRC has stressed the balance between economic
and security interests, required countries to operate a course correction
after years in which economic interests were prioritized, and led to a
degree of strategic ambiguity.

Since the early 2010s, when Obama formulated his "pivot to Asia"
policy, the feeling that the world was already too small for both
Washington and Beijing was tangible. Yet, in the second half of the decade it became clear that while the US, with Trump's hawkish approach,
was at the forefront of what seemed to be an anti-China crusade, other
countries followed the US. At times pressured by the White House, at
times concerned for their domestic security and values, other members
of the international community implicitly admitted that an acritical, two
decades-long neoliberal policy towards the PRC was no longer viable.
These countries all started to believe that the quality and intensity of

exchanges with China required stricter rules, although implementing this principle remains challenging. Authoritative commentators coined the phrase "new Cold War" to describe wide-spreading tensions in Sino-American and Sino-western relations and to highlight what, over the past five years, has clearly become a negative spiral in them. However, in some cases it remains to be seen whether there has been a real, substantial shift away from neoliberalism in these countries, and from a China policy dictated by economic rather than security interests.

This chapter seeks to unpack these themes by looking at different case studies. Most western countries could have provided meaningful examples, the three case studies included in this chapter were selected based on certain criteria. Both the UK, South Korea and Australia have been close diplomatic and military allies of the United States for decades; at the same time, the UK sits within the transatlantic bloc of the West, whereas Australia and South Korea, to different degrees, sit across the West and Asia; due to their geoeconomic and geopolitical history, the three countries have experienced meaningful interactions with both the US and China, and in recent years have made newsworthy policy adjustments. Prior to delving into these case studies, this chapter offers an academic discussion on the "new Cold War" to set the scene, and to indicate that due to the problematic interdependence between the US and China, this is a new type of cold war. The chapter also provides an update on the recent China policy of the United States.

A NEW COLD WAR? US–CHINA RELATIONS AFTER TRUMP

Between rapprochement in 1972 and the 2010s, US–China relations displayed systemic stability. It was always obvious to both parties that they were never going to forge a special relationship. Indeed, there were moments of high tension, whether during the Reagan administration or in the aftermath of the Tiananmen Square massacre, or in the 1995–96 Taiwan Strait Crisis. But in the past, both powers found it convenient to put differences aside for the sake of their national interest. With the Trump administration, however, the US became more impatient about its political and ideological differences with China, whereas Beijing since the beginning of Xi's presidency has appeared to be more inflexible to external input. Covid-19 certainly contributed to raising tensions. Trump blamed China for its spread, while Xi's zero-Covid campaign contributed to further isolating China. The Russian invasion of Ukraine in 2022 added to China's international isolation.

In the months prior to and following his election, many asked whether Biden was going to improve the relationship with China and unravel Trump's trade policies. Soon after Biden was sworn in, these hopes were dashed, and in less than one year Sino-American relations went from the fallout at the unproductive Anchorage Summit in Alaska, to the diplomatic boycott of the 2022 Winter Olympics in Beijing, and to exerting pressure on Beijing to take a stance against Russia in the Ukrainian crisis.

Although US athletes still attended the Olympic Games – another example of the tension between economic and security interests – the boycott was historic, as the only two previous major boycotts to have occurred in modern history are those of 1980 and 1984, and were a spill-over from the Cold War. The idea of a "new Cold War" has made inroads into the debate on US–China relations since the Trump adminis-tration, even though it remains contested. Journalists found the concept useful to describe a relationship marked by ideological and geopoliti-cal differences that seem irreconcilable. *The Economist* (2019) empha-sized the global spectrum that this relationship covers. It suggested that this might be "a new kind of cold war" and noted that "every domain, from semiconductors to submarines and from blockbuster films to lunar exploration" is becoming contested. Along similar lines, it was suggested that US–China relations resemble "two superpowers" that compete "across multiple geographic theatres (South Asia, Southeast Asia, Australia, Europe, Africa and Latin America) and multiple vectors (trade, investment, technology, espionage, international institutions, health policy, naval, air power, missiles and territorial disputes)" (Kemp 2020). Furthermore, they seek to bring "third countries into an alliance system" on their side – an aspect that is especially relevant to the case studies in this chapter. Other authoritative voices from the world of media made similar arguments, with realist scholars arguing that the geopolitical transition illustrated in the first chapter of this book is lead-ing to some kind of US–China "bipolarity"; indeed, "no other state is strong enough to serve as a competitor of these two" (Tunsjø 2018: 1).

There are some, however, who find this comparison far-fetched. Prominent Cold War historian Odd Arne Westad warned that this is "a rivalry of a different kind" where the "risk of immediate war is lower, and the odds of limited cooperation are higher" (2019: 93). In addition, he noted that China can live with the US's global predominance if it can achieve "regional dominance" – although, one wonders how the US can have global predominance without dominating the geoeconomically most important region of the next decades (*ibid.*: 91). Two US-based international politics experts added that "[w]ith analogical reasoning, people cling to superficial similarities and overlook the underlying differences. But it is often the underlying differences that really matter" (Ashford & Kroenig 2020). Meanwhile, Thomas Christensen has pointed out that current US–China competition lacks "a global ideological struggle", "separated economic blocs", and "opposing alliance systems" (2020: 7–8). Christensen was right, to an extent, when writing about this but recent developments like Covid-19 and Russia's invasion of Ukraine have accelerated a trend towards an international, systemic split.

A third group of scholars occupy the middle-ground, arguing that it is still too early to reach a conclusion on this issue, or that differences persist alongside similarities. Michael McFaul, former American ambassador to the Soviet Union, pointed out that while one should not define "today's great-power competition mechanically as another Cold War … ignoring parallels between US–Soviet relations in the last century and US–China relations in this century risks repeating some of our worst mistakes" (McFaul 2020: 8–9). Giulio Pugliese, instead, cautiously specified that while it might be premature to call this a Cold War, "China's assertiveness and the US maximalist pushback" are leading the relationship in that direction (2020: 8).

To this author, US–China relations resemble "a new type of Cold War". On the one hand, this is because of the geographically global, industrially transversal and militarily confrontational dynamic of US–China competition. The latter is ubiquitous because the US is a quasi-global, declining hegemon, whereas China is a rising power that "continues to be omnipresent throughout the globe in all walks of life" (Mascitelli 2019: 5). On the other hand, contemporary US–China competition remains "cold" to the extent that the two great powers have sought to avoid a military confrontation that could escalate into a major war. While economic interdependence is the main reason for restraint – together with nuclear weapons – as the previous chapters of the book have emphasized, it is also a major cause of tension: ultimately, this is a relationship characterized by forced cooperation and restrained competition. This duality inevitably also has an impact on US allies. The new Cold War puts those countries that are both US allies and China's partners in front of dilemmas and hard choices, especially where US diplomatic and military allies are involved, as the second part of this chapter shows.

CHALLENGES TO BIDEN'S STRATEGY OF DECOUPLING FROM CHINA

President Biden has not yet left a personal footprint or articulated a comprehensive American foreign policy doctrine. That said, from early on in the administration there has been certainty over two points: prioritizing China among other threats, and doing so through strengthening the relationship with allies to repair the damage caused by the Trump administration. These two elements are closely related. Compared to Obama and Trump, Joe Biden's China policy has sought to bring greater grand strategic coherence to the efforts of his predecessors. This approach to China is reflected in the Interim National Security Strategic Guidance; the launch of the Global Partnership for Infrastructure and Investment (GPII); and the US Innovation and Competition Act (2021).

In a provisional national security strategy, the Biden administration described the PRC as "the only competitor potentially capable of combining its economic, diplomatic, military, and technological power to mount a sustained challenge to a stable and open international system" (2021: 8). In continuity with Obama and Trump, Biden sees the US–China relationship as the most important one. Interestingly, Biden emphasized the centrality of alliances, stating that "one thing is certain: we will only succeed in advancing American interests and upholding our universal values by working in common cause with our closest allies and partners" (Biden 2021: iii). Consistent with this effort, Congress has been debating the US Innovation and Competition Act (2021) – approved in the Senate at the time of writing. The latter compels the current US administration to securitize industrial sectors such as semiconductors, supply chains, outer space investments and cybertech in relation to the economic-technological-military threat posed by China (S.1260 – United States Innovation and Competition Act of 2021). In this way, the US has adopted a whole-of-government approach to policy-making that implies coordination between different levers of power and between domestic security and foreign policy. By doing so – in addition to passing the CHIPS Act in support of the semiconductor industry – Washington has been taking a leaf out of China's book, seeking to imitate the benefits of state coordination over the strategic sectors of the country. Consistent with Biden's statement on the centrality of allies, S.3209 of the Act requires the US to lead towards "new technology policy partnerships focused on the shared interests of the world's technology-leading democracies"; and the secretary of state to "establish an interagency-staffed Technology Partnership Office" in cooperation with other departments of the US government, with the aim of pursuing American interests over "5G telecommunications", "semiconductor manufacturing", "biotechnology", "quantum computing", among others. This should be done by liaising with G7 and G20 members, the bill suggested.

The US Innovation and Competition Act should give legal backdrop to the PGII, originally named Build Back Better World (B3W). The B3W was presented at Biden's first G7 as US president in June 2021; it sought to deal with epochal global challenges and it did have a multinational character, as it requires cooperation with allies to work. Under the slogan of Build Back Better World, Biden effectively sought to leverage the pandemic to consolidate American influence in the West and to persuade US allies to join efforts in an anti-China coalition. The White House's factsheet emphasized that the B3W was "a values-driven, high-standard, and transparent infrastructure partnership led by major democracies" to support the developing world after the Covid-19 pandemic, and that its main areas of concern are "climate, health and health security, digital technology, and gender equity and equality" (White House 2021). Meanwhile, the Carbis Bay G7 Summit Communiqué emphasized values, standards and the centrality of the rules-based international order (G7 Cornwall 2021).

Was the B3W just a buzzword of an administration that wanted to make an impression soon after being sworn in? Or did the B3W encapsulate a grand strategic vision? The B3W was surrounded by uncertainty, from its reliance on private funding to the political resolve in a broad coalition. Yet, the vision behind it bears much strategic thinking and is in continuity with American grand strategy. Organizing a coalition of like-minded states is the key to future US–China and Sino-western relations. A few allies currently hold in their hands the outcome of the hegemonic competition between Washington and Beijing. Will they side with the former or the latter? Observing some of these countries in the coming years will provide us with a geopolitical thermometer of the US hegemony's state of health and China's rise to be a leading great power. In this regard, the B3W could be seen as an operation of order (re-)engineering to overcome the crisis of the LIO and, more specifically China and the BRI. De facto, the B3W sought to create a LIO 2.0; that is, a stricter layer of rules to protect next-generation industries and profitable investments from the Chinese state-led capitalism by using standards that Beijing does not want to comply with. Furthermore, it aimed at gathering resources to address the infrastructural gap of developing countries, an arena that China (through the BRI) sees as its own sphere of influence. This resembles what, in Chapter 3, was described as "positive decoupling". This, however, can only be achieved via a large coalition of states, because the economic stakes are too high for any country to decouple from China in isolation.

Biden "walked away" from the G7 summit in 2021 convinced that the group recognizes that Beijing is part of a growing threat to global democracy (Biden 2021b). However, it is unclear at this stage whether this strategy will be successful as European allies did not want to fully commit to this proposal. The G7 communiqué confirmed that members "will cooperate to address the challenge posed by China G7 Cornwall 2021", but only "where it is in our mutual interest" (G7 Cornwall 2021). Meanwhile, as a harsh reminder of the China conundrum, the media reported that Britain, the EU, Canada and Italy were not keen to pursue Biden's hard line towards Beijing.

During the G7 Summit 2022 held in Bavaria (Germany), however, the B3W was rebranded as the Partnership for Global Infrastructure and Investment (PGII), although the objectives and approach have not changed. Indeed, it was argued that this initiative is "a continuation and expansion of the Build Back Better World (B3W) initiative introduced by

Biden last year as a strategic alternative to China's Belt and Road (BRI)" (Rahman & Ahmad 2022). Consistent with the B3W, the White House confirmed that the US with the PGII seeks to "catalyze international infrastructure financing and development" under the same framework (White House 2022b). That said, the rebranding of the B3W only one year after its launch shows how complex Biden's attempt can be, and that Beijing's tight control of its industries allows China and the BRI to be more competitive and effective.

BRITAIN'S CHINA POLICY AFTER BREXIT: UNTOLD STRATEGIC AMBIGUITY

Since the handover of Hong Kong was completed in 1997, the UK's foreign policy towards the PRC has been characterized by efforts to compromise between economic and security interests. Throughout the New Labour era, Britain's China policy was informed by Tony Blair's "ethical foreign policy" and, towards the end of the 2010s, by *The UK and China: A Framework for Engagement* (FCO 2009). Both approaches highlighted that the UK hoped to have the "flexibility" to pick and choose how it wanted to handle Beijing (Brown 2011: 178). Far from being effective, this approach allowed the relationship to be predominantly shaped by "financial collaboration" more than anything else (Zhang 2019: 209). These were the premises for the Conservative–Liberal Democrat coalition (2010–15) led by David Cameron to conduct an explicitly neoliberal China policy. Those years were described by the chancellor George Osborne as the "golden era" in Sino-British relations, a slogan meant to welcome Xi Jinping's visit to the UK in 2015, and were characterized by an intensification of economic cooperation between London and Beijing. Important deals were made: London became the first western clearing centre for the renminbi; the UK was the first country in the West to allow a consortium of industries, within which the state-owned China National Nuclear Corporation (CNNC) featured to build the Hinkley Point C civil nuclear plant; finally, the UK also became the first western country to join the China-led Asian Infrastructure Investment Bank (AIIB) (Lockett & Hughes 2016). While these events – and the UK AIIB membership in particular – led the Obama administration to accuse London of "constant accommodation" with China, security "worries" about Hinkley Point C were "overruled" (Freeman 2019: 670; Thomas 2017: 690).

As Theresa May replaced Cameron at Downing Street the international environment around China was changing too because of worsening US–China relations. A Chinese official complained that during May's years in office the "level of enthusiasm" was not the same as the one experienced with the "Cameron Osborne team" (Ford & Kynge 2017). With a spiral of events between the summer of 2019 and the summer of 2020, which included reports of violation of civil and human rights in Hong Kong and Xinjiang, together with the row over Huawei's 5G, it was said the relationship went into "deep freeze" (Ford & Hughes 2020).

These events determined the current status quo in UK's China policy, but the United States played a major role in Boris Johnson's U-turn on Huawei, which would have been China's flagship investment in the country. It was reported that the British government admitted Huawei was banned due to "geopolitical" concerns and "huge pressure from President Donald Trump" (Helm 2020). This volatile international environment and the special relationship with the US provided, domestically, "momentum" for the British anti-China camp to become more vocal. Amidst this turmoil, the Integrated Review was issued by HM Government in 2021. The document described the PRC as the "biggest state-based threat to the UK's economic security" and argued that its military modernization and assertiveness threaten British interests in the Indo-Pacific (HM Government 2021: 29, 62–3). What these statements achieved was the alignment of the UK to US national security strategy. Indeed, with the Integrated Review Britain officially acknowledged that the world order was undergoing a geopolitical transition, characterized, among other things, by the return of great power competition. There exist profound differences with Cameron's 2015 national security strategy, which advocated for a deeper relationship with China (HM Government 2015: 58).

There is no doubt that in recent years the "golden era" between the UK and China has ended. But is it a substantial, long-term shift, or simply a tactical adjustment? While Johnson's national security strategy has balanced Cameron's unrealistic foreign policy towards the PRC, there continues to be a degree of ambiguity. The UK has been scrutinizing and debating Chinese investments and China's policies more rigorously; a healthy practice for a sovereign country. However, the economic relationship with Beijing has also continued as usual. Big interests have undermined the British government's new posture on China. Banks such as HSBC and Standard Chartered publicly supported the national security law that China imposed on Hong Kong during the summer of 2020 due to the stability that this will provide. Given the financial power of these private institutions, the UK government faces a major challenge; especially since these businesses are British but make much of their money overseas. Refraining their appetite for profits will require a creative mix of coercion and appeasement.

On the other hand, from a military and diplomatic perspective, the UK continues to signal its full commitment to its alliance with the US, as shown when it sent the aircraft carrier *HMS Queen Elizabeth* to the South China Sea during its first tour. However, it still acts ambiguously. When the trilateral pact for developing nuclear-powered submarines in Australia, AUKUS, was agreed with Canberra, London and Washington, Boris Johnson was very careful not to mention China in his speech, focusing on jobs for British workers as opposed to geostrategic objectives (Johnson 2021).

SOUTH KOREA'S CHINA POLICY: OFFICIAL STRATEGIC AMBIGUITY

The case of the Republic of Korea (ROK, or South Korea) is worth monitoring in the context of evolving relations between China and the world. Amidst the new Cold War between Washington and Beijing, understanding the posturing of Seoul could provide important lessons and predictions about future diplomatic pathways for other countries. As explained in a report published by Chatham House, the peculiarity of South Korea is that of enjoying "[d]eep historical and cultural ties with China that pre-date the emergence of the People's Republic of China in 1949", in addition to "geographical proximity, economic convergence and the mediating role" that China plays with the Democratic People's Republic of Korea (DPRK; North Korea) – the ROK's most pressing challenge (Nilsson-Wright & Jie 2021: 5). This makes the Korean case interesting: its elites will have to deploy fine-grained skills for navigating pressures stemming from their friendly relations with both the US and China, although the bond with the US is an official and long-standing one.

Since the early stages of the Cold War, South Korea has been tied to the US by a mutual defence treaty. This has granted "the right to dispose United States land, air and sea forces in and about the territory of the Republic of Korea"; its purpose has been to deter and respond to "an armed attack in the Pacific area on either of the Parties" (Mutual Defense Treaty Between the United States and the Republic of Korea; 1 October 1953). Based on this, the United States has stationed almost 30,000 troops in the country. While this is beneficial to Seoul's security in a region with different flashpoints, it also guarantees the US a forward base in the heart of East Asia.

South Korean foreign policy in the context of the Sino-American rivalry has been one of strategic ambiguity. Its aim is that of "not antagonizing China so that Korea can secure benefits from both Beijing and Washington – relying on the former for trade and the latter for its security interests" (Whan-Woo 2020). As Chatham House noted, this ambivalence is not so much about "balancing or hedging", rather it is an act of "selectively opting for policies that alternately or simultaneously involve cooperation (and occasionally conflict) with either or both partners" (Nilsson-Wright & Jie 2021: 16). Furthermore, such ambiguity stems from a tradition of constructing a "middle power" identity meant to pursue "non-alignment" and to "avoid being trapped in great power rivalries", not so different from the practices of other Asia states (*ibid.*: 18). The report also noted that South Korean governments, "whether conservative or progressive" have sought to manage cooperation with the US while "balancing the economic and security-related opportunities and challenges associated with a rising China" (*ibid.*: 5). This is a useful point, as one can infer from it that while the dilemmas and tensions between China and the West exert pressure on many countries, national governments have been able to adjust their postures based on their ideology and on the electoral agendas of the party in charge at any given point. Therefore, in South Korea – as much as everywhere else – centre-right coalitions are likely to display a more pro-US stance – although, this was clearly not the case for Cameron's government. In fact, Sino-Korean relations experienced a fallout during the deployment of the Terminal High Altitude Area Defence (THAAD) – an anti-ballistic missile defence platform – operational since 2017 and installed during the Park Geun-hye conservative presidency. The recent fluctuations in UK–China relations were avoided by democratic president Moon Jae-in who sought to balance the policy of his predecessor by making choices that pleased Beijing. Indeed, as it was reported Korea has not banned Huawei's 5G from the network of LG U+, the local operator; it has not endorsed Canada's Declaration Against Detention in State-to-State Relations; and is one of the few democracies that has not manifested its support for protesters in Hong Kong (Kim 2021).

Yet, it is worth asking whether the summer of 2021 became a watershed in recent Korean-American relations. First, at the Biden–Moon meeting in May, three important decisions were taken: in a highly symbolic gesture, Biden awarded the highest military recognition to a veteran of the Korean War who led troops against Chinese forces; the Revised Missile Guidelines was terminated together with the cap it imposed on the range of Korea's ballistic missiles; and a Korean-American joint statement on peace, stability and freedom of navigation around Taiwan and the South China Sea was issued (Kim 2021).

Second, in June 2021 South Korea joined the G7 in the UK as one of several guest countries – although Korea was not a signatory of the communiqué – when Biden launched his B3W. Korea's participation in the summit angered Beijing. China "nudged" Seoul ahead of the meeting. The Chinese foreign minister Wang Yi reminded his Korean counterpart Chung Eui-yong during a phone conversation that China and Korea are "friendly neighbours and strategic partners", and that China "strongly opposes the U.S. government's Indo-Pacific strategy, as it is full of Cold War thinking" (Kwon 2021).

This, however, begs the question: what has prompted the Moon administration to move closer to the United States? Based on the UK case study, there are two logical answers. Firstly, it might reflect domestic pressures from within the Democratic Party that advocate for a more hawkish China policy. This is not too different from what happened in the UK when a faction within the Conservative Party in the spring of 2021 pressed Boris Johnson to take a tougher stance on China. Secondly, this move might have stemmed from Moon's strict adherence to South

Korea's manual of strategic ambiguity and diplomatic correctness. For confirmation as to whether this is a gear shift, we will have to wait for further developments in the China policy of President Yoon Suk-yeol from the conservative People Power Party. Yoon won the March 2022 elections, a result that worries China. At this stage, however, it cannot be said to what extent Korea's strategic ambiguity remains "sustainable" as Sino-American tensions grow (Nilsson-Wright & Jie 2021).

SINO-AUSTRALIAN RELATIONS: A NEGATIVE SPIRAL

Australia is a very important case study when it comes to measuring the success or limits of China's engagement with the world. However, it is so for different reasons than the UK and South Korea examples. Unlike the UK case, China is Australia's first trading partner and the two countries have been tied into an economic relationship that has grown over the years. A senior advisor to Prime Minister Malcolm Turnbull described the relationship noting that "[i]t is hard to think of any two economies in the world that are more complementary" (Garnaut 2018). Yet, Australia has also been a close diplomatic and military ally of the US. For too long, it was argued, Canberra thought it could balance its relations with the two great powers. However, as early as 2016 two observers maintained that "this veneer of stability is misleading" because there is a void filled with "shifting ephemeral political trends driven by volatile emotions" rather than a "long-term strategic vision" (Brown & Bretherton 2016: 1). They seemed to warn that such a balance could not last for long. Indeed, not too differently from the end of the "golden era" in the UK, Sino-Australian relations unravelled in about five years. Since the second half of the 2010s a long list of factors has led to the "reset" in Australia's China policy (Garnaut 2018). During this time, different reports denounced CCP interferences and proselytizing efforts among "retired" influential Australian individuals. Since 2015, the Australian Security Intelligence Organisation (ASIO) warned Australian political parties of powerful donors being connected to the CCP. This was confirmed when China sought to leverage Australian prisoners in the PRC to obtain diplomatic gains; and threatened to harm the Labour Party by influencing the decisions of the Chinese community on the continent to convince Canberra to sustain a "bilateral extradition treaty". Although such turmoil was being widely reported in the media, the Turnbull administration commissioned a report on "foreign interference" which was published in 2017. Eventually, this led to a foreign interference bill being approved by the Australian parliament, as Turnbull commented that there had been "disturbing reports about Chinese influence" (BBC News 2018). As seen in other countries, especially in the UK, this "reset" – as Garnaut called it – caused a backlash among the academic and business community (Garnaut 2018). Nonetheless, in line with the UK, "[t]rust in China has fallen to a new record low": in 2021 only 16 per cent of Australians trusted China "to act responsibly in the world", a decrease of 7 per cent compared to 2020 (Kassam 2021: 4).

Ultimately, according to Rory Medcalf, this negative spiral of events comes down to what China wants from Australia. Medcalf included four items on the shopping list: because Australia is "a key US ally" in the Indo-Pacific, weakening the alliance contributes to China's strategic objective of weakening the US hegemonic foothold in the region; Canberra has "military, intelligence and capability secrets and technologies" that the PRC would benefit from; Australia is, from a soft-power viewpoint, a regional leader, and what Canberra says about China has an impact on others in the region; finally, Australia is "home to large communities of Chinese heritage" and Beijing wants to influence them (*ibid.*: 110). The Foreign Policy White Paper 2017 alluded to China as a security concern several times, although not explicitly. It stated that it opposed use of "coercive power" in the Indo-Pacific or in the East China Sea and Taiwan Strait (Foreign Policy White Paper 2017: 3, 47). At the same time, it ambiguously stated that the Australian government remained "committed to strong and constructive ties with China" (*ibid.*: 4). Nonetheless, the paper expressed concerns for "the unprecedented pace and scale of China's [revisionist] activities" in the South China Sea (46–7). Yet, a commentator from the think tank Asia Society noted that because of the economic crisis that followed Covid-19, the deterioration in Sino-Australia relations, the unilateralism in US foreign policy during the Trump era and the crisis in US–China relations, it was time for Canberra to update the 2017 white paper – and that de facto this is already happening (Maude 2020).

More recently, relations between China and Australia deteriorated for two reasons. First, Canberra supported a call for a global inquiry into the origins of Covid-19 requested by the US (CNBC 2020). This led Beijing to impose tariffs and restrictions on imports from the continent, including coal, beef, cotton and wine, putting great pressure on the Australian business community. China was then outraged by the launch of AUKUS. This pact was seen by many as Australia stepping up to a greater security commitment in the Indo-Pacific on the side of the US. However, the three partners, and especially Australia and the UK, were not clear about what AUKUS was meant to be. Intuitively, most people saw in it a geostrategic move to counter the growing assertiveness of China in the western Pacific. This makes sense, but it is not how Prime Minister Boris Johnson presented AUKUS in September 2021. Johnson's speech clearly emphasized that AUKUS was going to create jobs in Britain and, rather confusingly, he noted that the pact is "equally momentous for any other state to come to its aid", as if Australia was facing an imminent military threat. The speech of Prime Minister Morrison, likewise, did not provide any additional insights into what exactly AUKUS is. He noted that the world "is becoming more complex" and that existing partnerships between the three countries have to be taken "to a new level … to engage, not to exclude; to contribute, not take; and to enable and empower, not to control or coerce". If AUKUS remains in between a framework for technological cooperation and geostrategy in the Indo-Pacific, it also remains unclear whether this pact is a novelty and to what extent AUKUS is a game-changer (Global Times 2021). The three parties are already allied within several frameworks, including Five Eyes. In the *Global Times* China reacted by arguing that "nuclear-powered submarines are designed to be strategic striking tools" and that this means it is very clear what the pact is about. It warned that "China will certainly punish it with no mercy" should Canberra continue this escalation. Given that at this stage AUKUS seems to be a pact that bears diplomatic symbolism rather than practical implications, China is probably more concerned about Australia sending a signal that continues to maintain a strong partnership with both Washington and London.

Each of the three case studies, with their different national peculiarities, have followed a similar pattern. All of them have demonstrated a degree of strategic ambiguity amidst growing geopolitical tensions between the US and China. Furthermore, in all cases the UK, South Korea and Australia, have made steps that indicate renewed support for the United States in different ways and to different degrees. Indeed, South Korea appears to have sought to handle this conundrum in a more calculated manner; whereas the UK and Australia appear to have adopted an abrupt shift away from China. But as Australia has been facing the ire of Beijing and its commercial restrictions, the UK has managed to keep the economic relationship unaltered while siding with the US in regional military affairs. Furthermore, the three cases showed that when the country is ruled by a centre-left or centre-right party – or coalition – this might affect the stance towards Beijing and how the economy-security conundrum is managed – although, this is not necessarily always the case.

To be fair, ambiguity has characterized US foreign policy towards China. This lies at the bottom of the new type of cold war between the two great powers. Many pundits do not agree with parallels being drawn between today and the Cold War of the twentieth century. Regardless, the ambiguous strategy that characterizes the China policy of several western countries, while not being ideal, may signal that those geopolitical tensions could be contained for the next decade.

Conclusion

There are four main lessons that stem from this exploration of Sino-western relations, in addition to some more tangible recommendations that can be inferred from these. This book has showed that it is not possible to discuss or even think about the modern or contemporary history of China without considering its relationship with the West. Since the First Opium War, China's trajectory has been influenced by the West, sometimes for good, sometimes for ill. European, American and Japanese imperialism, and open-door policies have contributed to China's desire for catching up and playing hard in a competitive international system of states. The US, since 1972, has actively supported efforts of the PRC to become a prosperous country. Likewise, there is no modern history of the West without discussion of China. Without the meeting between Mao and Nixon, the Cold War might have lasted longer; without Deng Xiaoping's reformist agenda, the LIO would not have been global from an economic point of view.

Currently, both China and the West, especially the US, are locked in a problematic interdependence which has led them to consider options for decoupling and recovering national sovereignty over different aspects of economic and social life. Indeed, while the liberal order has trapped the West into a China conundrum, the more China engages with this order the more it faces dilemmas between competing interests. If current diplomatic quarrels between China and the West worries us a lessening of such interdependence through decoupling could lead to a degree of geopolitical stability, because interdependence remains a source of tensions.

Another major historical lesson concerns the need to look at history in the *longue durée*. In 1972 Nixon and Mao were agreeing on a process of "rapprochement" between Washington and Beijing, which led to "normalization" under the Carter administration, and which allowed both powers to survive through events that shook the fundaments of the relationship – Tiananmen Square (1989) and the Taiwan Crisis (1995–96). By the standards of contemporary western-centric pundits, this seems like an age ago. Yet, in only a few decades we have managed to move from the Cold War to a time of potential order-unravelling and to the brink of a new Cold War, or the return of great power politics at the very least. Here, there are lessons for the West to the extent it has been unable to maintain the post-Second World War order despite occupying a position of strength in it. Part of the problem seems to be the tragedy of history – to paraphrase Mearsheimer – by which winners prefer a "winner takes it all" approach and seek to achieve the ultimate victory. But in an anarchic international system, there cannot be a permanent victory, only a temporary success. Since the end of the Cold War the international order unravelled quickly and the illusion of the "end of history" has prevented many from seeing this coming.

A third lesson concerns the LIO. The "civilizationism" of the West made many believe that the LIO represented the "normal" in world politics and the geopolitical spaces that fell outside of it were few, or did not count that much, and were described as rogue or unruled states. Yet, when the post-Cold War "hangover" finally ended, the rise of China, together with the economic success of Asia with its own socio-political culture, has demonstrated that the LIO has spread unevenly across a very diverse world order. With the decline of US unipolarism and the rise of China more specifically, the demarcation between orders will only become more visible.

The fourth lesson is that the objective success story of the PRC in the past 40 years, coupled with the economic crisis faced in the West, has served as a reminder that markets can fail; that national interests still matter; and that the state needs to apply greater strategic supervision to its national economy. Neoliberalism is no longer in fashion as it was in the 1990s. This is good news, because several countries are seriously thinking of the benefits of whole-of-government and whole-of-society approaches to different challenges. Furthermore, although few people will acknowledge this, it is also thanks to the success of capitalism with Chinese characteristics that we are looking into alternatives. However, two challenges remain ahead. On the one hand, we do not know yet how much of the rhetoric about greater state supervision of the sensitive sectors of society will become a reality. On the other hand, in a time of economic crisis, social turmoil and the need for a more diffused control of people due to Covid-19 and made possible through information technology, governments and citizens must be careful when hoping for greater supervision by the state. With more coordination between the levers of state power, opposition to increased centralization will be fundamental.

Drawing lessons is an essential part of any organization with a long-term objective and a strategy, be it an institution or a company. It is a major component in the academic training of the military all over the world, whereas big businesses dedicate hours of meetings to reflect on what has worked and what has not. However, lessons are an assessment of the past; what the West needs is a way forward in its relationship with China.

To begin with, any recommendation should acknowledge two facts. First, the unravelling of Sino-western relations of recent years has been, to an extent, a healthy event. Indeed, as the reader of this book will understand, Sino-western relations as they were in the 1990s and 2000s were simply unrealistic and could not last. Recognizing that something was wrong and in need of rebalancing is already a major step forward. However, the current political frenzy – although healthy – makes it difficult to develop a balanced strategy. Second, there is no perfect solution to the China conundrum. The endemic tension of the LIO in addition to China's resilient political system does not allow the luxury of a smooth China strategy. This leaves governments with a degree of freedom for manoeuvre depending on their ideological background and electoral agenda. Some will prioritize engagement with China, while others will prioritize security.

After such a self-reflective, inward-looking moment, any China policy should be honest, pragmatic but bold, rather than simply an ideological one. Being honest and pragmatic means that the West should avoid picking fights over issues China does not intend to negotiate on and that are highly symbolic, such as Taiwan; to acknowledge the damage of nineteenth- and twentieth-century imperialism; not to expect to interfere in Chinese affairs; but also to understand that negotiation will be possible only in some areas, and to be realistic about it. Yet, the

West must pursue engagement where China is willing to negotiate, and firm containment where China is unwilling to do so. China's approach to international negotiations is one of "hardening the hard, and softening the soft". Simply put, countries who find their relationship with the PRC to be imbalanced should consistently apply a policy of reciprocity, to retaliate where Beijing restricts the space for freedom and to expand where Beijing is willing to compromise. The West should be bold and stand strong over issues that are under its full political and legitimate control, from Chinese investments on sensitive and strategic industries to western companies' activities in China. This presents a challenge, but it is an area where governments have the right to do so.

Another suggestion is to recognize that, frustratingly, a major part of the solution to the China conundrum does not lie in the foreign policy of western countries, but in domestic policy. The primary reason for China's success in the West is the latter's long-term trajectory of financial stagnation. This prevents countries from handling their trade relationship with China from a position of strength. If it is true that "China has more money than God", as a commentator from *Forbes* put it, western countries need to access a share of that wealth. Bringing this problem under control will allow countries to assess with the necessary time and more objectively the benefits and the risks of Chinese investments; it will also allow them to consider more carefully the opportunity of delocalization and investments to China.

Some western countries, due to their colonial past, enjoy access to a rich network of partners and allies. This needs to be leveraged in the making of a China policy. Considering that some of these partners – Singapore, some ASEAN members, South Korea – are going through a major effort of strategic ambiguity, countries like the UK, the US, or EU members, will greatly benefit from consistently exchanging ideas on best diplomatic practices. As seen during the fast development of the first wave of Covid-19, technical diplomatic communication between states over common challenges appears to be slow and limited. Second, and following from the previous point, this effort of coordination will be essential if every country wants to be prepared to fend off the PRC's efforts to divide and rule on the international scene. Furthermore, this seems a logical start for agendas on greater technological and geopolitical coordination such as the B3W launched by President Biden or similar initiatives that will surely emerge in the future.

The LIO, even at the apex of the US unipolar moment was always one order among competing – perhaps still developing – orders. China's "common prosperity" campaign and Biden's B3W signal that we might be heading towards a less blurred world order where the liberal order will coexist with a separate China-led order.

As two China-based scholars point out, "[o]ne person's 'wolf warrior foreign policy' and 'debt trap diplomacy' may be another person's pursuit of a 'harmonious world' and 'community of common destiny'" (Grydehøj & Su 2022: 74). This is a highly controversial comment, and certainly one that serves China's propaganda. Yet, this statement also contains a truth that is hard to digest for westerners: the LIO exists and the US is seeking to prevent its erosion; there is also the PRC with a grand strategy that accepts the LIO when convenient, but when the LIO does not work in its interests it seeks to de-westernize China. We are witnessing a clash of two competing societal models at an international level. As is often the case in history, it is power that will determine who is right and who is wrong. However, five decades after the historic meeting between Mao and Nixon, the hope is that diplomacy will rediscover a degree of pragmatism which for too long has been neglected.

References

Allison, J. & A. Alexander 2009. "The uses and misuses of uneven and combined development: an anatomy of a concept". *Cambridge Review of International Affairs* 22(1): 47–67.

Acharya, A. 2014. *The End of the American Order*. Cambridge: Polity Press.

Arrighi, G. 2007. *Adam Smith in Beijing: Lineages of the Twenty-First Century*. London: Verso.

Australian Government 2017. 2017 Foreign Policy White Paper. November. https://www.dfat.gov.au/sites/default/files/2017-foreign-policy-white-paper.pdf.

Baker, G. 2019. "In 1989, the U.S. decided to let Beijing get away with murder". *Wall Street Journal*, 31 May. https://www.wsj.com/articles/in-1989-the-u-s-decided-to-let-beijing-get-away-with-murder-11559311545.

Barnett, T. 2004. *The Pentagon's New Map: War and Peace in the Twenty-First Century*. New York: Putnam.

Belt and Road Forum for International Cooperation 2017. Full Text: Vision and actions on jointly building Belt and Road (2). 10 April. http://2017.beltandroadforum.org/english/n100/2017/0410/c22-45-2.html.

Best Global Brands (2020). https://www.interbrand.com/best-global-brands/.

Biden, J. 2021a. Statement of President Joe Biden on Senate Passage of the U.S. Innovation and Competition Act. The White House. 8 June. https://www.whitehouse.gov/briefing-room/statements-releases/2021/06/08/statement-of-president-joe-biden-on-senate-passage-of-the-u-s-innovation-and-competition-act/.

Biden, J. 2021b. Remarks by President Biden in Press Conference. The White House. Cornwall, UK, 13 June. https://www.whitehouse.gov/briefing-room/speeches-remarks/2021/06/13/remarks-by-president-biden-in-press-conference-2/.

Biscop, S. 2021. *Grand Strategy in 10 Words: A Guide to Great Power Politics in the 21st Century*. Bristol: Bristol University Press.

Boer, R. 2021. *Socialism with Chinese Characteristics: A Guide for Foreigners.* Singapore: Springer Nature.

Breslin, S. 2004. "Beyond diplomacy? UK relations with China since 1997". *British Journal of Politics and International Relations* 6(3): 409–25.

BRICS Leaders Xiamen Declaration Xiamen 2017. BRICS 2017. China, 4 September. www.brics.utoronto.ca/docs/170904-xiamen.pdf.

Brown, K. 2011. "Britain's relations with China under New Labour: engagement and repulsion?" In O. Daddow & J. Gaskarth (eds), *British Foreign Policy: The New Labour Years*, 170–87. London: Palgrave Macmillan.

Brown, K. 2017. *China's World: What Does China Want?* London: I. B. Tauris.

Brown, K. & H. Bretherton 2016. "Australian relations with China and the USA: the challenge of grand strategies". *Australian Journal of International Affairs* 70(1): 1–5.

Bush, G. H. W. & B. Scowcroft 1998. *A World Transformed.* New York: Knopf.

Bush, G. W. 1999. "Governor George W. Bush, 'A Distinctly American Internationalism'". Ronald Reagan Presidential Library, Simi Valley, California, 19 November. https://www.mtholyoke.edu/acad/intrel/bush/wspeech.htm.

Bush, G. W. 2001. "Remarks and a question-and-answer session with the American society of newspaper editors". The American Presidency Project. 5 April. https://www.presidency.ucsb.edu/documents/remarks-and-question-and-answer-session-with-the-american-society-newspaper-editors-3.

Castells, M. 2010. *The Rise of the Network Society.* Chichester: Wiley-Blackwell.

ChinaFile 2013. Document 9: A ChinaFile Translation. 8 November. https://www.chinafile.com/document-9-chinafile-translation.

China Power Team 2017. "How well-off is China's middle class?". *China Power.* 26 April, updated 30 September 2021. https://chinapower.csis.org/china-middle-class/.

Christensen, T. 2020. "No new Cold War: why US–China strategic competition will not be like the US–Soviet Cold War". *The Asan Institute for Policy Studies.* September.

Climate Action Tracker 2021. "China". 28 October. https://climateactiontracker.org/countries/china/.

Clinton, W. 2000. "Full text of Clinton's speech on China trade bill". *Institute for Agriculture and Trade Policy.* 9 March. https://www.iatp.org/sites/default/files/Full_Text_of_Clintons_Speech_on_China_Trade_Bi.htm.

Coons, C. 2019. "Remarks by U.S. Senator Chris Coons: The Nixon Forum on U.S.–China Relations". Wilson Center, 18 October. https://www.wilsoncenter.org/article/remarks-us-senator-chris-coons-the-nixon-forum-us-china-relations.

Council on Foreign Relations n.d. "U.S.–Russia Nuclear Arms Control

1949–2021". https://www.cfr.org/timeline/us-russia-nuclear-arms-control.

Davin, D. 2013. *Mao: A Very Short Introduction*. Oxford: Oxford University Press.

Deng, X. & Q. Hu 1980–81. Remarks on Successive Drafts of the "Resolution on Certain Questions in the History of our Party since the Founding of the People's Republic of China". March 1980–June 1981. En.People.Cn/Dengxp/Vol2/Text/B1420.Html.

Duhigg, C. & K. Bradsher 2012. "How the U.S. lost out on iPhone work". *New York Times*, 22 January. https://www.nytimes.com/2012/01/22/business/apple-america-and-a-squeezed-middle-class.html.

Economy, E. 2017. "Why China is no climate leader". Politico. 12 June. https://www.politico.com/magazine/story/2017/06/12/why-china-is-no-climate-leader-215249/.

Economy, E. 2018. *The Third Revolution: Xi Jinping and the New Chinese State*. New York: Oxford University Press.

Elliot, J. 2002. *Some Did It for Civilisation, Some Did It for Their Country: A Revised View of the Boxer War*. Hong Kong: The Chinese University Press.

Ellis-Petersen, H. 2021. "India criticised over coal at Cop26 – but real villain was climate injustice". *The Guardian*, 14 November. https://www.theguardian.com/environment/2021/nov/14/india-criticised-over-coal-at-cop26-but-real-villain-was-climate-injustice.

European Chamber of Commerce in China (ECCC) 2021. Business Confidence Survey 2021: European Business in China. file:///C:/Users/k1466458/Downloads/RB_BCS_EN.pdf.

Farrell, H. & A. Newman 2021. "Weaponized interdependence". In D. Drezner, H. Farrell & A. Newman (eds), *The Uses and Abuses of Weaponized Interdependence*. Washington, DC: Brookings Institution Press.

Fenby, J. 2017. *Will China China Dominate the 21st Century?* Cambridge: Polity Press.

Flint, C. 2017. *Introduction to Geopolitics*. Third edition. Abingdon: Routledge.

Foot, R. 2005. "Prizes won, opportunities lost: the US normalization of relations with China, 1972–1979". In W. Kirby, R. Ross & G. Li (eds), *Normalization of U.S.–China Relations: An International History*. Cambridge, MA: Harvard University Press.

Ford, J. & J. Kynge 2017. "Beijing signals end of China–UK 'golden age'". *Financial Times*, 6 January. https://www.ft.com/content/4ab22b66-d42d-11e6-9341-7393bb2e1b51.

Ford, J. & L. Hughes 2020. "UK–China relations: from 'golden era' to the deep freeze". *Financial Times*, 14 July. https://www.ft.com/content/804175d0-8b47-4427-9853-2aded76f48e4.

Ford, L. & R. Hass 2021. "Democracy in Asia". The Brookings Institution, 22 January. https://www.brookings.edu/articles/democracy-in-asia/.

Frankopan, P. 2015. *The Silk Roads: A New History of the World*. London: Bloomsbury.

Freedman, L. 1998. "Introduction: the revolution in strategic affairs". *The Adelphi Papers* 38(318): 5–10.

Freeman, C. 2019. "Constructive engagement? The US and the AIIB". *Global Policy* 10(4): 667–76.

Fukuyama, F. 1995. "Confucianism and democracy". *Journal of Democracy* 6(2): 22–33.

Garnaut, J. 2018. "Australia's China reset". *The Monthly*, August. https://www.themonthly.com.au/issue/2018/august/1533045600/john-garnaut/australia-s-china-reset.

Gibson, R. 2019. Testimony of Rosemary Gibson, Senior Advisor, The Hastings Center and Author, "China Rx: Exposing the Risks of America's Dependence on China for Medicine". Before the U.S.-China Economic and Security Review Commission "Exploring the Growing U.S. Reliance on China's Biotech and Pharmaceutical Products". July 31. https://www.uscc.gov/sites/default/files/RosemaryGibsonTestimonyUSCCJuly152019.pdf.

Gill, B. 2007. *Rising Star: China's New Security Diplomacy*. Washington, DC: Brookings Institution Press.

Global Times 2021. "AUKUS to bring 'nuclear-powered submarine fever' across globe". *Global Times*, editorial, 16 September. https://www.globaltimes.cn/page/202109/1234459.shtml.

Goldstone, J. 2008. *Why Europe? The Rise of the West in World History, 1500–1850*. Boston, MA: McGraw Hill.

Gong, G. 2011. "What China wants: China's climate change priorities in a post-Copenhagen world". *Global Change, Peace & Security* 23(2): 159–75.

Greer, T. 2019. "Xi Jinping in translation: China's guiding ideology". *Palladium*, 31 May. https://palladiummag.com/2019/05/31/xi-jinping-in-translation-chinas-guiding-ideology/.

Gungwu, W. 2009. "Rationalizing China's place in Asia". In A. Reid & Y. Zheng (eds), *Negotiating Asymmetry: China's Place in Asia*. Singapore: NUS.

G7 Cornwall 2021. Carbis Bay G7 Summit Communique, June. https://www.g7uk.org/wp-content/uploads/2021/06/Carbis-Bay-G7-Summit-Communique-PDF-430KB-25-pages-3-1.pdf.

HM Government 2021. Global Britain in a competitive age. https://assets.publishing.service.gov.uk/government/uploads/system/uploads/attachment_data/file/975077/Global_Britain_in_a_Competitive_Age-_the_

Integrated_Review_of_Security__Defence__Development_and_Foreign_
Policy.pdf

Hancock, T. 2018. "China's relentless export machine moves up the value
chain". *Financial Times*, 23 September. https://www.ft.com/content/cdc
53aee-bc2e-11e8-94b2-17176fbf93f5.

Harding, H. 1992. *A Fragile Relationship: The United States and China since
1972*. Washington, DC: Brookings Institution Press.

Harris, P. 2011. "Peace, security and global climate change: the vital role of
China". *Global Change, Peace & Security* 23(2): 141–5.

Harris, R. 1959. "China and the world". *International Affairs* 35(2): 161–9.

Harvey, D. 2003. *The New Imperialism*. Oxford: Oxford University Press.

Hass, R. 2021. "Assessing China's 'common prosperity' campaign". Brookings
Institution, 9 September. https://www.brookings.edu/blog/order-from-
chaos/2021/09/09/assessing-chinas-common-prosperity-campaign/.

Heilmann, S. 2017. *China's Political System*. Lanham, MD: Rowman &
Littlefield.

Helm, T. 2020. "Pressure from Trump led to 5G ban, Britain tells Huawei". *The
Guardian*, 18 July. https://www.theguardian.com/technology/2020/jul/18/
pressure-from-trump-led-to-5g-ban-britain-tells-huawei.

House of Commons Foreign Affairs Committee 2019. "China and the Rules-
Based International System. Sixteenth Report of Session 2017–19". 4 April.
https://publications.parliament.uk/pa/cm201719/cmselect/cmfaff/612/612.
pdf.

Hugill, P. 2009. "The American challenge to British hegemony, 1861–1947".
Geographical Review 99(3): 403–25.

Ikenberry, G. 2011. *Liberal Leviathan: The Origins, Crisis, and Transformation
of the American World Order*. Princeton, NJ: Princeton University Press.

Jacques, M. 2009. *When China Rules the World: The Rise of the Middle Kingdom
and the End of the Western World*. New York: Penguin.

Johnson, B. 2021. PM Statement on AUKUS Partnership, 15 September.
Prime Minister's Office, London. 15 September. https://www.gov.uk/
government/speeches/pm-statement-on-aukus-partnership-15-september-
2021.

Johnson, C. 2002. *Blowback: The Costs and Consequences of American Empire*.
London: Sphere.

Johnson, K. & R. Gramer 2020. "The great decoupling". *Foreign Policy*, 14
May. https://foreignpolicy.com/2020/05/14/china-us-pandemic-economy-
tensions-trump-coronavirus-covid-new-cold-war-economics-the-great-
decoupling/.

Joint Communiqué of the United States of America and the People's Republic of China 1972. Shanghai, People's Republic of China. https://digitalarchive. wilsoncenter.org/document/121325.

Joint Communiqué on the Establishment of Diplomatic Relations between the People's Republic of China and the United States of America 1978. Embassy of the People's Republic of China in the United States of America. 16 December. https://www.mfa.gov.cn/ce/ceus/eng/zmgx/zywj/t36256.htm.

Jones, B. 2021. "Major power rivalry and the management of global threats". Council on Foreign Relations Discussion Paper Series on Managing Global Disorder No. 7. November. https://cdn.cfr.org/sites/default/files/report_pdf/ Jones_MajorPowerRivalry.pdf.

Jones, L. & S. Hameiri 2020. "Debunking the myth of 'debt-trap diplomacy'". Chatham House, 19 August. https://www.chathamhouse.org/2020/08/ debunking-myth-debt-trap-diplomacy/6-conclusion-and-policy- recommendations.

Kalantzakos, S. 2018. *China and the Geopolitics of Rare Earths.* New York: Oxford University Press.

Kassam, N. 2021. Lowy Institute Poll 2021. 23 June. https://poll.lowyinstitute. org/files/lowyinsitutepoll-2021.pdf.

Kaufman, A. 2010. "The 'Century of Humiliation', then and now: Chinese perceptions of the international order". *Pacific Focus* 25(1): 1–33.

Kemp, J. 2020. "United States and China enter a new cold war". *Reuters*, 27 July. https://www.reuters.com/article/uk-global-politics-kemp-idUKKCN24 S11F.

Kennedy, P. 1987. *The Rise and Fall of Great Powers: Economic Change and Military Conflict from 1500 to 2000.* New York: Random House.

Khanna, P. 2019. *The Future is Asian: Commerce, Conflict, and Culture in the 21st Century.* New York: Simon & Schuster.

Kim, S. 2021. "Takeaways from the Biden–Moon summit: three observations on China". The Rand Blog, 7 June. https://www.rand.org/blog/2021/06/ takeaways-from-the-biden-moon-summit-three-observations.html.

Kissinger, H. 1971. Steps Towards Augmentation of Travel and Trade Between the People's Republic of China and the United States. Nixon Library, 25 March. Shttps://cdn.nixonlibrary.org/01/wp-content/uploads/2017/01/ 19110034/HAK-RN-Augmentation-of-Travel-and-Trade-with-PRC- 3.25.71-HAK-Box-86-Folder-1.pdf.

Kissinger, H. 2014. *World Order.* New York: Penguin.

Knickmeyer, E. 2021. "Costs of the Afghanistan war, in lives and dollars". AP News, 17 August. https://apnews.com/article/middle-east-business- afghanistan-43d8f53b35e80ec18c130cd683e1a38f.

Kota, S. & T. Mahoney 2020. "Loss of the industrial commons is an existential threat to US prosperity". Indiana University Manufacturing Policy Initiative. https://policyinstitute.iu.edu/doc/mpi/2020/kota-mahoney-2020.pdf.

Kroenig, M. 2020. *The Return of Great Power Rivalry: Democracy Versus Autocracy from the Ancient World to the U.S. and China*. New York: Oxford University Press.

Kroenig, M. & E. Ashford 2020. "Is this the beginning of a new Cold War with China?". Cato Institute, 31 July. https://www.cato.org/commentary/beginning-new-cold-war-china.

Kuo, L. 2021. "Xi Jinping's crackdown on everything is remaking Chinese society". *Washington Post*, 16 November. https://www.washingtonpost.com/world/asia_pacific/china-crackdown-tech-celebrities-xi/2021/09/09/b4c2409c-0c66-11ec-a7c8-61bb7b3bf628_story.html.

Kwon, M.-y. 2021. "G7's rivalry with China complicates Korea's balancing act". *Korea Times*, 4 February. www.koreatimes.co.kr/www/nation/2021/07/120_310415.html.

Lake, D., L. Martin & T. Risse 2021. "Challenges to the liberal order: reflections on international organization". *International Organization* 75(2): 225–57.

Lake, A. 1993. "Remarks of Anthony Lake, assistant to the president for national security affairs: 'From containment to enlargement'". 21 September. Washington, DC: The White House. https://babel.hathitrust.org/cgi/pt?id=mdp.39015051567645;view=1up;seq=3.

Lee, K.-F. 2018. *AI Superpowers: China, Silicon Valley, and the New World Order*. Boston, MA: Houghton Mifflin Harcourt.

Lee, Y. 2021. "China's economy could double in size by 2035 – and surpass the U.S. along the way". CNBC. 26 February. https://www.cnbc.com/2021/02/26/china-has-a-good-chance-of-doubling-gdp-by-2035-says-bank-of-america.html.

Lenin, V. 1939. *Imperialism, the Highest Stage of Capitalism*. New York: International Publishers.

Leoni, Z. 2021. *American Grand Strategy from Obama to Trump: Imperialism After Bush and China's Hegemonic Challenge*. Cham, CH: Springer Nature.

Lewis, L. 2021. "Companies prepare for a 'selective decoupling' with China". *Financial Times*, 10 October. https://www.ft.com/content/5ca525f7-cb40-468a-a294-5938d11af6a5

Lockett, H. & J. Hughes 2021. "UK becomes second-largest offshore renminbi clearing centre". *Financial Times*, 28 April. https://www.ft.com/content/9fd82346-0cf2-11e6-b41f-0beb7e589515.

Mahbubani, K. 2020. *Has China Won? The Chinese Challenge to American Primacy*. New York: Public Affairs.

Mai, J. & G. Rui 2021. "Viral blogger hailed China's 'profound revolution', but the state may disagree". *South China Morning Post*, 3 September. https://www.scmp.com/news/china/politics/article/3147548/viral-blogger-hailed-chinas-profound-revolution-state-may.

Maina, S. 2017. "Transsion Holdings is China's largest phone exporter and Africa's leading phone seller". *Techweez*, 21 November. https://techweez.com/2017/11/21/transsion-sales-h1-2017/.

Mascitelli, B. & M. Chung 2019. "Hue and cry over Huawei: Cold war tensions, security threats or anticompetitive behaviour?" *Research in Globalization* 1: 1–6.

Mauldin, J. 2019. "China's grand plan to take over the world". *Forbes*, 12 November. https://www.forbes.com/sites/johnmauldin/2019/11/12/chinas-grand-plan-to-take-over-the-world/?sh=a5a1ffb5ab5d.

McFaul, M. 2020. "Cold War lessons and fallacies for US–China relations today". *The Washington Quarterly* 43(4): 7–39.

McKinsey Global Institute 2019. China and the World: Inside the Dynamics of a Changing Relationship. https://www.mckinsey.com/~/media/mckinsey/featured%20insights/china/china%20and%20the%20world%20inside%20the%20dynamics%20of%20a%20changing%20relationship/mgi-china-and-the-world-full-report-feb-2020-en.pdf.

McMaster, H. 2020. "How China sees the world: and how we should see China". *The Atlantic*, May. https://www.theatlantic.com/magazine/archive/2020/05/mcmaster-china-strategy/609088/.

Medcalf, R. 2019. "Mapping a multipolar future: the contest for the Indo-Pacific". *Global Asia* 14(4): 61–2.

Mertha, A. 2009. "'Fragmented authoritarianism 2.0': political pluralization in the Chinese policy process". *China Quarterly* 200: 995–1012.

Milanovic, B. 2020. "The clash of capitalisms: the real fight for the global economy's future". *Foreign Affairs* 99(1): 10–21.

Miller, T. 2017. *China's Asian Dream*. London: Zed Books.

Mitter, R. 2016. *Modern China: A Very Short Introduction*. Oxford: Oxford University Press.

Moore, S. 2011. "Strategic imperative? Reading China's climate policy in terms of core interests". *Global Change, Peace & Security* 23(2): 147–57.

Morrison, S. 2021. Address: AUKUS - CANBERRA, ACT. Prime Minister of Australia. 16 September. https://www.pm.gov.au/media/address-aukus-canberra-act

Morrison, W. 2019. "China's economic rise: history, trends, challenges, and implications for the United States". *Congressional Research Service* RL33534. https://sgp.fas.org/crs/row/RL33534.pdf.

Morton, S. & J. Olenik 2004. *Japan: Its History and Culture*. Fourth edition. New York: McGraw-Hill.

Mutual Defense Treaty Between the United States and the Republic of Korea 1953. 1 October. https://www.usfk.mil/Portals/105/Documents/SOFA/H_Mutual%20Defense%20Treaty_1953.pdf

Ni, V. 2021. "China urges developed countries to take the lead in cutting out coal". *The Guardian*, 15 November. https://www.theguardian.com/world/2021/nov/15/china-urges-developed-countries-to-take-the-lead-in-cutting-out-coal.

Nilsson-Wright, J. & Y. Jie 2021. "South Korean foreign policy innovation amid Sino-US rivalry strategic partnerships and managed ambiguity". Chatham House, July. https://www.chathamhouse.org/sites/default/files/2021-07/2021-07-22-south-korean-foreign-policy-innovation-nilsson-wright-et-al.pdf.

Nixon, R. 1967. "Asia after Vietnam". *Foreign Affairs* 46(1): 111–25.

Norris, W. 2016. *Chinese Economic Statecraft: Commercial Actors, Grand Strategy, and State Control*. Ithaca, NY: Cornell University Press.

Office of the Secretary of Defense 2021. "Military and Security Developments Involving the People's Republic of China". 3 November. https://media.defense.gov/2021/Nov/03/2002885874/-1/-1/0/2021-CMPR-FINAL.PDF.

Palley, T. 2012. "The economic and geo-political implications of China-centric globalization". New America Foundation. https://www.newamerica.org/economic-growth/policy-papers/the-economic-and-geo-political-implications-of-china-centric-globalization/.

Pei, M. 2020. "China's expensive bet on Africa has failed". Nikkei Asia, 1 May. https://asia.nikkei.com/Opinion/China-s-expensive-bet-on-Africa-has-failed.

Phoenix Weekly 2015. "Chinese overseas investment hindered by lack of experience, political opposition in host countries". *Global Times*, 14 September. https://www.globaltimes.cn/content/942349.shtml.

Pomeranz, K. 2000. *The Great Divergence: China, Europe, and the Making of the Modern World Economy*. Princeton, NJ: Princeton University Press.

Pugliese, G. "COVID-19 and the Reification of the US–China 'Cold War'". *Asia-Pacific Journal* 18(5): 1–10.

Quinn, A. & M. Cox 2007. "For better, for worse: how America's foreign policy became wedded to liberal universalism". *Global Society* 21(4): 499–519.

Rapoza, K. 2017. "China's government has more money than you can imagine". *Forbes*, 10 October. https://www.forbes.com/sites/kenrapoza/2017/10/10/chinas-government-has-more-money-than-you-can-imagine/?sh=733a436a63c4.

Rapp-Hooper, M. *et al*. 2019. "Responding to China's complicated views on international order". Carnegie Endowment for International Peace. 10 October. https://carnegieendowment.org/2019/10/10/responding-to-china-s-complicated-views-on-international-order-pub-80021.

Reality Check Team 2019. "How much of Europe does China own?". BBC News, 20 April. https://www.bbc.co.uk/news/world-47886902.

Rees, V. 2019. "Swine fever in China raises concern over heparin supply for US". *European Pharmaceutical Review*, 2 August. https://www.european pharmaceuticalreview.com/news/95829/swine-fever-in-china-raises-concern-over-heparin-supply-for-us/.

Reuters Staff 2019. "China's rare earth supplies could be vital bargaining chip in U.S. trade war". Reuters, 30 May. https://www.reuters.com/article/us-usa-china-rareearth-explainer-idUSKCN1T00EK.

Rice, C. 2000. "Promoting the national interest". *Foreign Affairs* 79(1): 45–62.

Richard, M. 2020. "After the White Paper: Australian foreign policy in a COVID-19 world". Asia Society, 10 September. https://asiasociety.org/australia/after-white-paper-australian-foreign-policy-covid-19-world.

Rogers, J. *et al*. 2020. "Breaking the China supply chain: how the 'Five Eyes' can decouple from strategic dependency". Henry Jackson Society. https://www.dica.org.au/wp-content/uploads/2020/05/Breaking-the-China-Chain.pdf.

Rolf, S. 2021. *China's Uneven and Combined Development*. Cham, CH: Springer Nature.

Roy, D. 1994. "Singapore, China, and the 'soft authoritarian' challenge". *Asian Survey* 34(3): 231–42.

Schmidt, C. 2018. "Values and democracy in East Asia and Europe: a comparison". *Asian Journal of German and European Studies* 3(1): 1–16.

Schneider-Petsinger, M. 2020. "Prospects for transatlantic cooperation and the global trade system". Chatham House, 11 September. https://www.chathamhouse.org/2020/09/reforming-world-trade-organization/summary.

Schondelmeyer, S. 2021. Strategic Assessment of the Resilience of the U.S. Drug Supply with Lessons from the Pandemic & Recommendations for Moving Beyond. Committee on Homeland Security and Governmental Affairs United States Senate Congress of the United States. https://www.hsgac.senate.gov/imo/media/doc/Testimony-Schondelmeyer-2021-05-19-11.pdf

Serhan, Y. & K. Gilsinan 2020. "Can the West actually ditch China?" *The Atlantic*, 24 April. https://www.theatlantic.com/politics/archive/2020/04/us-britain-dependence-china-trade/610615/.

Shambaugh, D. 2013. *China Goes Global: The Partial Power*. Oxford: Oxford University Press.

Shambaugh, D. 2016. "Are China's multinational corporations really multinational?". In *The China Reader: Rising Power*. Sixth edition. New York: Oxford University Press.

Shambaugh, D. 2020. "Introduction". In D. Shambaugh (ed.), *China and the World*. Oxford: Oxford University Press.

Sherwell, P. 2020. "Who needs democracy? China's 400 million millennials prefer iPhones". *Sunday Times*, 24 October. https://www.thetimes.co.uk/article/chinas-young-watch-trump-and-breathe-a-sigh-of-relief-they-dont-have-democracy-r7bc3g2wf.

Silove, N. 2016. "The pivot before the pivot: U.S. strategy to preserve the power balance in Asia". *International Security* 40(4): 45–88.

Smith, N. 2006. "The geography of uneven development". In B. Dunn & H. Radice (Eds), *100 Years of Permanent Revolution: Results and Prospects*. London: Pluto Press.

Standoff at Tiananmen 2012. "Document of 1989: President Bush's Secret Letter to Deng Xiaoping". www.standoffattiananmen.com/2012/06/document-of-1989-president-bushs-secret.html.

Stephens, P. 2008. "Crisis marks out a new geopolitical order". *Financial Times*, 9 October. https://www.ft.com/content/0ed4a750-961e-11dd-9dce000077b07658.

Storey, H. 2021. "Can Biden's Build Back Better World compete with the Belt and Road?". The Lowy Institute, 20 July. https://www.lowyinstitute.org/the-interpreter/can-biden-s-build-back-better-world-compete-belt-and-road.

Swagel, P. 2010. "The cost of the financial crisis: the impact of the September 2008 economic collapse". PEW Economic Policy Group Briefing Paper #18. http://www.pewtrusts.org/~/media/assets/2010/04/28/cos tofthecrisisfinal.pdf.

Tang, D. 2021. "China ready to cut out 'tumours' of celebrity and capitalism". *The Times*, 31 August. https://www.thetimes.co.uk/article/china-vows-to-crush-celebrity-and-capitalism-in-profound-revolution.

Tao, W. 2022. *A History of China–US Relations (1911–1949)*. Singapore: Springer Nature.

The Economist 2011a. "All change". *The Economist*, 10 December. https://www.economist.com/asia/2011/12/10/all-change.

The Economist 2011b. "No change". *The Economist*, 10 December. https://www.economist.com/asia/2011/12/10/no-change.

The Economist 2011b. "Shades of grey". *The Economist*, 10 December. https://www.economist.com/leaders/2011/12/10/shades-of-gr.

The Economist 2012. "The world's shifting centre of gravity". *The Economist*, 28 June. https://www.economist.com/graphic-detail/2012/06/28/the-worlds-shifting-centre-of-gravity.

The Economist 2019. "A new kind of cold war". *The Economist*, 18 May. https://www.economist.com/leaders/2019/05/16/a-new-kind-of-cold-war.

The Economist 2020. "Covid-19 is teaching hard lessons about China-only supply". *The Economist*, 29 February. https://www.economist.com/china/2020/02/29/covid-19-is-teaching-hard-lessons-about-china-only-supply-chains.

The Economist 2021. "Chinese youth Young Chinese are both patriotic and socially progressive". *The Economist*, 23 January. https://www.economist.com/special-report/2021/01/21/young-chinese-are-both-patriotic-and-socially-progressive.

The Economist 2021. "Biden's new China doctrine". *The Economist*, 17 July. https://www.economist.com/leaders/2021/07/17/bidens-new-china-doctrine.

The National People's Congress of the People's Republic of China 2009. "China's Position on the Copenhagen Climate Change Conference". 20 May. www.npc.gov.cn/zgrdw/englishnpc/Special/CombatingClimateChange/2009-08/25/content_1515282.htm.

The State Council Information Office of the People's Republic of China 2015. "China's Military Strategy (full text)". 27 May. english.www.gov.cn/archive/white_paper/2015/05/27/content_281475115610833.htm.

The State Council Information Office of the People's Republic of China 2019. "Full Text: China's National Defense in the New Era". 24 July. english.www.gov.cn/archive/whitepaper/201907/24/content_WS5d3941ddc6d08408f502283d.html

The World Bank 2020. "China". https://data.worldbank.org/country/CN (accessed 26 December 2021).

The World Bank n.d. "Military expenditure (current USD) – United States". Chinahttps://data.worldbank.org/indicator/MS.MIL.XPND.CD?locations=US-CN.

The World Bank 2021. "Foreign direct investment, net inflows (BoP, current US$) – China, Euro area, United States, Japan, Germany". https://data.worldbank.org/indicator/BX.KLT.DINV.CD.WD?locations=CN-XC-US-JP-DE.

The White House 2021. "President Biden and G7 Leaders Launch Build Back Better World (B3W) Partnership". Factsheet, 12 June. https://www.whitehouse.gov/briefing-room/statements-releases/2021/06/12/fact-sheet-president-biden-and-g7-leaders-launch-build-back-better-world-b3w-partnership/.

The White House 2000. "National Security Strategy 2000". 1 December. nssarchive.us/national-security-strategy-2000-2/.

The White House 2021. "Interim National Security Strategic Guidance 2021". https://www.whitehouse.gov/wp-content/uploads/2021/03/NSC-1v2.pdf.

Thomas, T. 2014. *China: Military Strategy: Basic Concepts and Examples of its Use*. Amazon.

Tonby, O. *et al.* 2019. "Asia's future is now". McKinsey Global Institute. https://www.mckinsey.com/~/media/mckinsey/featured%20insights/asia%20pacific/asias%20future%20is%20now/asias-future-is-now-final.pdf.

Tooze, A. 2014. *The Deluge: The Great War and the Remaking of Global Order 1916–1931*. London: Penguin.

Trotsky, L. 2008. *History of the Russian Revolution*. Chicago, IL: Haymarket Books.

Tunsjø, Ø. 2018. *The Return of Bipolarity in World Politics: China, the United States, and Geostructural Realism*. New York: Columbia University Press.

Tzeng, F.-W. 1991. "The political economy of China's coastal development strategy: a preliminary analysis". *Asian Survey* 31(3): 270–71.

United Nations Department of Economic and Social Affairs n.d. "Jointly building the "Belt and Road" towards the Sustainable Development Goals". https://www.un.org/en/desa/jointly-building-"belt-and-road"-towards-sustainable-development-goals.

United Nations Framework Convention on Climate Change n.d. "The Paris Agreement". https://unfccc.int/process-and-meetings/the-paris-agreement/the-paris-agreement.

UNCTAD 2020. "Developing countries pay environmental cost of electric car batteries". https://unctad.org/news/developing-countries-pay-environmental-cost-electric-car-batteries.

US Congress 1979. H.R. 2479 – Taiwan Relations Act. 96th Congress (1979–80). https://www.congress.gov/bill/96th-congress/house-bill/2479.

Wallerstein, I. 1979. *The Capitalist World-Economy*. New York: Cambridge University Press.

Wang, D. 2021. *The United States and China: A History from the Eighteenth Century to the Present*. Second edition, Lanham, MD: Rowman & Littlefield.

Wei, L. 2019. "Towards economic decoupling? Mapping Chinese discourse on the China–US trade war". *Chinese Journal of International Politics* 12(4): 519–56.

Westad, A. 2019. "The sources of Chinese conduct: are Washington and Beijing fighting a new Cold War?" *Foreign Affairs* 98(5): 86–95.

Westcott, B. & G. Steve 2018. "How George H. W. Bush became Beijing's 'old friend' in the White House". CNN, 2 December. https://edition.cnn.com/2018/12/01/asia/george-h-w-bush-china-intl/index.html.

Whan-woo, Y. 2020. "US–China row calls Korea's strategic ambiguity into question". *Korea Times*, 3 February. https://www.koreatimes.co.kr/www/nation/2020/08/120_294275.html.

White, H. 2013. *The China Choice: Why We Should Share Power*. Oxford: Oxford University Press.

Wyne, A. 2020. "How to think about potentially decoupling from China". *The Washington Quarterly*. 43(1): 57.

Xi, J. 2021. Full text of Xi Jinping's speech on the CCP's 100th anniversary. Nikkei Asia. 1 July. https://asia.nikkei.com/Politics/Full-text-of-Xi-Jinping-s-speech-on-the-CCP-s-100th-anniversary.

Xi, J. & D. Trump 2017. "Remarks by president Trump and president Xi of China at state dinner. Beijing". The White House, 9 November. https://www.whitehouse.gov/ briefings-statements/remarks-by-president-trump-and-president-xi-of-chinaat-state-dinner-beijing-china/.

Yeung, Y., J. Lee & G. Kee 2009. "China's Special Economic Zones at 30". *Eurasian Geography and Economics* 50(2): 222–40.

Zhang, L.-Y. 2018. "Green bonds in China and the Sino-British collaboration: more a partnership of learning than commerce". *British Journal of Politics and International Relations* 21(1): 207–25.

Zhou, C. 2019. "Why is emerging global superpower China still categorised as a 'developing' country?". ABC News, 10 April. https://www.abc.net.au/news/2019-04-11/why-china-is-still-categorised-as-a-developing-country/10980480.

Zoellick, R. 2005. "Whither China? From membership to responsibility". National Committee on United States – China Relations, 21 September. https://www.ncuscr.org/sites/default/files/migration/Zoellick_remarks_notes06_winter_spring.pdf.

Index